Hemponomics

Unleashing the Power of Sustainable Growth

Scott Sondles,

HempStrong Co-founder

DEDICATION

This book is dedicated to my biggest fan, my mom. I would also like to give a shout out to all moms that have to put up with unruly sons, we mean well and you are appreciated.

CONTENTS

"There are two additional strengths of Sondles's book that I would like to mention. First, it includes an introduction to hemp's important place in world and American history. When you get done with the book you have to wonder how the textbook writers could ignore this crop in their books. The second strength of the book is that the author has a good sense of Austrian economics when it comes to politics, public policy, war, and even monetary theory, deflation and the Austrian business cycle theory. "

– Dr. Mark Thornton, Ludwig Von Mises Institute

Preface

I was in college studying finance & economics when the 2008 financial bubble hit. At the time I was too busy enjoying college life to pay much attention, but by the time my junior year rolled around I began looking toward my future and asking questions. My dad had just lost his job in the insurance business and I had become extremely interested in the 2008 housing bubble. I wanted to know everything about it. Why it happened? Is it going to happen again? Who predicted it? Did they profit and why? What does economic history teach us about future depressions?

I surprisingly didn't find the answers to my questions in my economic classes so I started educating myself online. I found many of the answers I was looking for and uncovered hundreds of more questions. *The two biggest things I learned were to always question the status quo and to always do your own research.* It has been my focus on answering questions that mattered the most to me and questioning the status quo that has led me to industrial hemp.

I became aware of the hemp industries in Canada, China,

and all of Europe during the summer before my last semester of college. All of these countries had distinguished a clear difference between marijuana and hemp and had allowed their farmers to grow hemp for fiber and seed. My first interest in the hemp industry was hemp clothing and from there I realized the potential for using hemp in foods, plastics, textiles, and cosmetics. I also realized that I was going to need a career after graduating from the University of Kentucky and industrial hemp could provide multiple opportunities to do *meaningful work*. Upon graduation I co-founded a company called HempStrong Brands in order to bring innovative hemp products to market and help influence the way Americans farm and manufacturer.

HempStrong is a consumer products company that launches hemp products under the HempStrong family of brands. We are currently in the body care market with plans to come out with hemp supplements in 2014. We believe that by educating people on the benefits of hemp and developing America's hemp markets, we can be successful in changing the way Americans look at hemp. Current hemp laws in America say farmers must apply for permits that are granted by the DEA (Drug Enforcement Agency), but unfortunately the DEA has been unwilling to work with rural communities. We think its time that America start developing its own hemp industry and get the DEA out of the business of regulating America's biggest agriculture opportunity. Hemp has negligible quantities of THC (psychoactive drug in marijuana) and will only give the user a headache if they tried to smoke it.

Many people wrongly believe that hemp is the male plant and that marijuana is the female version of cannabis sativa. This is a misunderstanding however and both male and female forms of hemp have negligible quantities of THC. Marijuana and hemp are from the same family of plants similar to how a poodle and a wolf are both members of the canine family of animals. Users that consume hemp foods or apply hemp cosmetics have virtually zero risk of failing a drug test due to the low THC content. Hemp farmers in North America are also committed to the TestPledge program that guarantees hemp has negligible quantities of THC. Hemp is not a drug issue, it's a jobs and sustainability issue.

Around the same time I envisioned HempStrong I began drafting this book. I knew I was going to be entering the hemp industry and wanted to be able to summarize all the information I had absorbed into an easy to read book. This book would not of been possible if it wasn't for the countless researchers and hemp authors that came before me. The following pages will engulf you into the history of the hemp industry, the prohibition theory, the benefits of industrial hemp, and what industries are prepared to profit upon the reintroduction of industrial hemp. The last chapter I dive into the HempStrong story and our vision.

I hope my readers enjoy this book as much as I have enjoyed putting it together. I look forward to developing the American hemp industry with you and can't wait till the day American farmers can once again grow industrial hemp.

–   Scott Sondles

Chapter 1: History of Hemp

"I think a plant that can be grown organically, has low water requirements, is pest resistant, can't be used as a drug, has the potential to be the cornerstone of America's bioeconomy, and can be used in over 25,000 products should be outlawed." – Said no famous person ever

"Make the most of the Indian hemp seed, and sow it everywhere!" - George Washington –Note to the gardener, Mount Vernon, 1794

Beginning

Hemp is a variety of cannabis sativa and was one of the first crops domestically cultivated. Since its beginning hemp has been an essential staple crop and up until the mid 19th century it was the most traded commodity in the world.

It is believed that the earliest known fabrics were made of hemp fiber in Eastern Europe and Asia around 8000 BC. It was during this time that the first civilizations were being constructed around agriculture communities and by 4000 BC it has been shown that the Chinese had started using the hemp seeds for food. Besides clothing and food, hemp's most important use to our ancestors was rope. The pharaohs of Egypt used hemp rope to maneuver their stone blocks into place and Pharaoh Alchanaten was buried with hemp cloth in his tomb. Around 1100 BC the City of Carthage controlled the Mediterranean Sea mainly due to the use of hemp in ship's ropes and sails. Greek historian Herodotus even claimed around 450 BC that "hemp garments are as fine as linen."[1]

The next hemp breakthrough came around 100 AD when the Chinese discovered how to produce paper from hemp and mulberry. This was done underneath the Han Dynasty and it was this discovery that gave Asian cultures a leg up in preserving information and knowledge.[2] By the 8th century the process of making paper from hemp had made it all the way to Arabia and Persia through trade and warfare.

Over the next few generations the hemp paper trade would continue to spread west toward Samarkand and Baghdad. A few generations later the Moorish culture (Muslims) would introduce the first paper mills in Europe. The first mills in Europe were located in Spain and Sicily during the 10th century and would later spread to Germany by 1400. Many historians have argued that the Moorish culture and the development of hemp paper mills empowered Europe to climb out of the dark and gloomy Middle Ages. For example, the Moorish capital of Cordoba during the 10th century had a population of 500,000 and had 70 libraries that held an estimated 500,000 books. In comparison, London England at the time had a population of around 20,000 with the majority being illiterate.[3] The Moors wanted Cordoba to rival Baghdad and Constantinople in intellectual thought and followed the teachings of Mohammad who claimed 'the scholar's ink is holier than the martyr's blood' and 'that seeking knowledge is required of every Muslim.'[4] By bringing paper (large portion made from hemp cellulose fibers) to Europe the Moors were successful in protecting knowledge and allowed future scholars to build upon their own triumphs in math, science, agriculture, and health care.

Paper derived from hemp encouraged innovations in European countries and the invention of the printing press combined with hemp made paper started the printing revolution of the 15th century. The printing revolution spurred on education and increased wealth throughout Europe. Although the Far East at one time was the center of knowledge, they were years behind the European printing technology. The availability of hemp paper and the creation of the printing press played a huge role in the democratization of knowledge. This event in history can easily be compared to what the Internet has done for our learning capacities in recent years. In the same century, Johann Gutenberg printed Bibles on hemp paper that still remain to this day. Before Europeans began using hemp for paper they had to use animal skins that were not economically feasible for large books. Previous attempts to print bibles would use as many as 300 sheep hides.[5]

The advancement of the arts was also spurred on by the development of hemp markets. Before hemp canvas was created artists would have to paint or draw over their previous works since they couldn't afford the expensive new animal skins. The development of hemp canvases allowed artist to spread their wealth and create a plethora of masterpieces. The word canvas actually comes from the word cannabis and many of the oil paints used during this time were derived from hemp oil.[6]

When searching for the New World in 1485 Christopher Columbus sailed using only the strongest hemp sails and rope. He even carried extra hemp seed to cultivate if they became stranded and needed a good source of nutrition. It is estimated that each one of Columbus's ships carried over 80 tons of hemp material.

Francois Rabelais, Benedictine monk and author during the Renaissance period only had good things to say about hemp, "Without it (hemp) millers could neither carry wheat, nor any other kind of corn, to the mill; nor would they be able to bring back from thence flour, or any other sort of meal whatsoever. Without it, how could the papers and writs of lawyers' clients be brought to the bar? Seldom is the mortar, lime or plaster brought to the workhouse without it. Without it how should the water be got out of the draw well? In what case would tabellions, notaries, copists, makers of counterparts, writers, clerks, secretaries, scriviners, and such like persons be without it? Were it not for it, what would become of the toll-rates and rent-rolls? Would not the noble art of printing perish without it? Whereof could the chassis or paper windows be made? How should the bells be rung?"[7]

In 1563, Queen Elizabeth imposed strict laws regarding the farming of hemp. She demanded all landowners with over sixty acres of land to grow hemp or pay a fine of five British pounds. A year later King Philip of Spain would follow the Queen's policy and gave orders to grow hemp throughout the Spanish Empire (Argentina to as far North as Oregon). Hemp was at the center of every economy and was necessary for maintaining the security and safety of each country. Hemp is the strongest natural plant fiber known to man and was essential for the sails and rigging of the redesigned voyaging ships. These redesigned ships were equipped with tons of hemp textiles and allowed Europeans to brave the oceans instead of being land locked as in centuries before. When old hemp sails, textiles, and ropes were worn out paper manufacturers would then buy these goods to make their own products. One can easily make the argument that before the mid 19th century hemp was as important to economies as oil is to our generation.

Wild hemp was already growing in North America when the European settlers arrived in the New World. Historians believe that either early explorers from China brought the hemp seeds to North America or migrating birds from the Bering Strait brought the seeds over. When American colonist first landed in Jamestown, the Virginia Company ordered all farmers to grow hemp for the crown. Many reports show that the Puritans of Jamestown were not enthusiastic about growing hemp, but the motherland made hemp cultivation mandatory for security reasons.

England was not the only country in the New World that was demanding hemp from the colonies. Jean Talon, French Quebec's colony minister would commandeer all thread textiles that the colonist possessed and would demand that they buy the thread back from him with hemp. Talon would also supply the farmers with the initial hemp seed and the first hemp farmers would then be forced to compensate Talon during harvest time.

Around 1630 Thomas Budd from Pennsylvania wrote a book called *Good Order Established in New Jersey and*

Pennsylvania. In the book Budd establishes the importance of growing industrial hemp and flax in the northeast. Budd hoped that by growing hemp the colonist would be able to increase the production of textiles that could then be exported to England.[8]

In 1631 hemp cultivation laws were passed in Massachusetts and a year later Connecticut would follow. In some states hemp was so valued it was used as a legal tender and farmers paid taxes with hemp. When the Virginia governor protested the surplus of tobacco being produced in his colony, the British leaders wrote him back encouraging him to grow hemp as opposed to tobacco.

Russia soon became associated as having the highest quality hemp in the world. They produced 90% of the hemp Great Britain imported and around 80% of the total hemp consumed by the New World. Even though the Russians processed the best hemp, the British controlled the sea and thus the hemp trade. Each British ship needed 60 to 100 tons of hemp every other year and the British had to import the majority of this material. The ruling class in Russia was quite happy to supply the British with hemp fibers in return for gold. Hemp was the fabric of choice for the shipping industry due to its durability and ability to withstand the punishment from the sea.

The colonies of England were encouraged to grow hemp, but they were not encouraged to produce hemp textiles. The British wanted to transport the raw hemp materials back to England so they could provide jobs for the poor and then resell the finished hemp goods back to the colonies. This policy also enforced the colonial dependency to the crown and is a great example of one of the many *mercantilist* policies that the British government used to harass the colonies. In Boston during 1705 one ton of hemp would be given six English pounds if exported to Britain.[9] Even with this policy in place very little Colonial hemp made it back to the mother country and England purchased the majority of their hemp from the Baltic region.

As colonial hemp production increased, immigrants from Ireland started to arrive in the colonies where they would teach the art of weaving hemp fibers. This small event in history helped the colonist become more independent from British goods and helped bring about the American Revolution. In 1734 Connecticut began offering 20 shillings for "well wrought canvas or duck fit for use, of thirty-six yards in length and 30 inches wide, and weighting not less than 45 pounds, made of well-dressed, water-rotted hemp or flax."[10]

What is Mercantilism?

In the last section I used the term mercantilist or mercantilism to describe economic policies that were forced onto the colonist by the British King. Most people who keep up with the news have at least heard of the term "crony capitalism," but not to many people have heard of the term mercantilism. It is a word that has been around for centuries, but has been cast aside by mainstream media and replaced with "crony capitalism." I believe this is wrong and gives capitalism and the resulting free markets that are created in a capitalist society a bad name. Capitalism is the single greatest idea that the human race has ever created and will play a crucial roll as we build a more sustainable economy.

At its roots capitalism is the idea of using free markets to move a society forward and increase living conditions. Instead of depending on free markets, "crony capitalism" depends on the relationship between big business and big governments. By its very nature so called "crony capitalism" participants do not seek free markets at all and thus should not be labeled capitalism. When big business and big government get together its called mercantilism. The British developed the mercantilist system during the 17th and 18th century, but its policies can still be seen in today's economy.

Those who have studied the American Revolution understand that the American colonist seceded from the British due to the mercantilist policies that were being forced onto them by the King. The exporting of hemp materials to England was just a small example of these policies, but the majority of mercantilist policies involved unnecessary taxation. In essence entrepreneurs and businessmen led the revolt against the British only after suffering through the British economic policies that only benefited the elite. John Hancock himself was a famous entrepreneur who did his best to smuggle goods into the colonies in order to avoid the mercantilist taxes and fines.

After we won our independence not all Americans wanted to get rid of the mercantilist policies that had led to our revolt. A small group of politicians and businessmen wanted to use these same policies to benefit themselves now that they were in control. This group didn't see anything wrong with mercantilism besides the fact that they weren't the ones who were reaping the rewards from its policies. These mercantilist believed in connecting rich businessmen to the government, having a powerful central government, high tariffs to protect the business industries, and a central bank to help finance all of their political goals. Since the founding of our country we have been fighting these economic policies and today it is the root of our economic problems and the reason for the excessive inequality in America.

There are many different definitions of mercantilism, but the best definition I have found and the one I'm going to use came from the famous economist Murray Rothbard. In his book The Logic of Action he wrote mercantilism is "a system of statism which employs economic fallacy to build up a structure of imperial state power, as well as special subsidy and monopolistic privilege to individuals or groups favored by the state." Take a minute to let that marinate, it should sound pretty familiar to our current political culture. Many have correctly drawn comparisons of mercantilism to fascism, corporatism, and crony capitalism.

This is important to point out because the hemp industry has been both positively and negatively impacted by mercantilist policies enacted by our government. Most importantly readers should be aware that we currently live in a society that is still dominated by the mercantilist policies that depend on big government and big business. Throughout the rest of this book you will see me reference mercantilism in replace of the term crony capitalism.

By 1776 almost all the colonies had passed laws encouraging the cultivation of industrial hemp. Virginia actually began fining the farmers who did not obey the hemp laws and hemp mills would soon hire lobbyist to educate the public about their industry. That same year Thomas Paine published *Common Sense*, where he wrote "hemp flourishes even to rankness."

Hemp was essential to our fight for independence and was second to no other American asset. Hemp was not just used during the fight for independence, but leading up to the

American Revolution many of the political pamphlets and newspapers that were passed out were printed on hemp paper.

Thomas Jefferson drafted the Declaration of Independence on Dutch hemp paper, the second draft was also written on hemp paper and the final draft, which was signed by the founding fathers, was copied onto animal parchment. Thomas Jefferson would later state the following regarding hemp; "Plough the ground for it early in the fall & very deep. If possible plough it again in Feb. before you sow it, which should be in March. A hand can tend 3 acres of hemp a year. Tolerable ground yields 500 lb to the acre. You may generally count on 100 lb for every foot the hemp is over 4 feet high. A hand will break 60 or 70 lb a day, & even to 150. lb. If it is to be divided with an overseer, divide it as it is prepared.. To make hemp seed, make hills of the form & size of cucumber hills, from 4 to 6 feet apart, in proportion to the strength of the ground. Pinch about a dozen seeds into each hill in different parts of it. When they come up thin them to two. As soon as the male plants have shed their farina, cut them up, that the whole nourishment may go to the female plants. Every plant thus tended will yield a quart of seed. A bushel of good brown seed is enough for an acre."[11]

George Washington also grew hemp and many of his own garments were made from hemp fiber. His personal tailors; John and Betsy Ross were well schooled in how to handle hemp textiles. There are multiple stories regarding who made the first American flag or what it was made from, but many believe Betsy Ross made the first flag and it was made from hemp. Even if the first flag wasn't made from hemp, the rope that raised the flag to the top of Independence Hall on July 8, 1776 was made from hemp fiber.

Adam Smith, the most important economic thinker during this time wrote about the hemp industry in his well-known economic book, *Wealth Of Nations* (1776). When encouraging free trade between nations he states, "The capitals of the British manufacturers who work up the flax and **hemp** annually imported from the coasts of the Baltic, are surely very useful to the countries which produce them. Those materials are a part of the surplus produce of those countries which, unless it was annually exchanged for something which is in demand there." When writing about the roundabout trade between Americans, British, and Russians Smith writes, "If the flax and **hemp** of Riga are purchased with the tobacco of Virginia, which had been purchased with British manufactures, the merchant must wait for the returns of two distinct foreign trades before he can employ the same capital in re-purchasing a like quantity of British manufactures. If the tobacco of Virginia had been purchased, not with British manufactures, but with the sugar and rum of Jamaica which had been purchased with those manufactures, he must wait for the returns of three...Three times a greater capital must in both cases be employed, in order to exchange a certain value of British manufactures for a certain quantity of flax and **hemp**, than would have been necessary, had the manufactures and the flax and **hemp** been directly exchanged for one another."[12] Smith would also go on to mention hemp when discussing the Mercantile System (similar to crony capitalism) that had started in England and had worked its way over to America.

Edward Antil wrote the first known book on hemp in 1789 and called it *Observations On the Raising and Dressing of Hemp*. He has been quoted saying "hemp is one of the most profitable productions the Earth furnishes in northern climates; as it employs a great number of poor people in a very advantageous manner, if its manufacture is carried on properly: It ... becomes worthy of the serious attention of every trading man, who truly loves his country." Two years later hemp paper mill owner Ben Franklin printed the first American magazine article regarding the cultivation of hemp. It should also be noted that the kite that Franklin flew during his famous lightning experiment was attached to hemp string, "Franklin was safely ensconced in a shed when he attracted lightning with a key tied to a kite. He watched the lightning raise the hairs on the hemp kite string as it traveled downward into the Earth. Lemay says Franklin couldn't resist reaching out to touch the hemp and, as you'd expect, he got a slight shock."[13]

Kentucky soon became the destination for hemp farmers and in 1792 its legislature signed into law a tax of twenty-dollars per ton on any hemp that was imported from out of state. At one point Kentucky had over 160 factories that manufactured cordage, bagging, and rope. In the same year President Washington would incorporate a 10% protective duty on hemp in order to promote domestic hemp cultivation. He claimed hemp was "a necessity" and wanted farmers to grow hemp over tobacco. Alexander Hamilton, the first Secretary of the Treasury and the godfather of mercantilism in America played a big part in influencing Washington's tariff decision. Hamilton believed in the mercantilist policies of high tariffs, big government, banking cartel, and business cartel. These policies would soon be adopted by Kentucky congressman and hemp farmer Henry Clay and would eventually become the foundation of the Republican Party led by Lincoln.

Leading up to the War of 1812 mercantilism was taking over the country and more extreme protective policies were being introduced in Congress. These policies were aimed to protect certain manufacturing industries, with an emphasis on hemp. When President Madison was asked about protective tariffs he stated that he did not support such tariffs as a general policy, but specific manufacturing industries (hemp) did need these tariffs since they were vital to having a strong national defense. There is no doubt that Henry Clay played an influential part in Madison's stance since the hemp farmer had adopted the mercantilist policies that Hamilton had preached.

Hemp War of 1812

American Minister to Russia: John Quincy Adams

The year was 1809 and James Madison had just been inaugurated as the 4th president of the United States. One of the first actions taken by President Madison was appointing John Quincy Adams (JQA) to the position of American minister to the Russian czar, Alexander I. Three months after setting sail (under hemp sails) from South Carolina, JQA landed in Russia on October 23, 1809. Winter was approaching fast and in a few days Kronstadt harbor would be locked in a solid sheet of ice.

Once settled into his new home JQA was extremely successful in making an impression on the 32-year-old monarch. Alexander I and JQA began taking numerous walks together and would often converse in French about European problems and what life in America was like. It was this relationship that gave American merchant vessels access to Russian ports. The American ships were all seeking to purchase hemp cordage and sail in the Baltic.

At the time Russia was allied with Napoleon (who was fighting the British) and was given orders to halt trade with all neutral countries. After multiple reports of Great Britain and American ships being seen in the Kronstadt harbor (harbor for St. Petersburg), Napoleon took his Grand Army of around half a million men and on June 25, 1812 invaded Russia. Napoleon was not going to allow the British access to Russia's hemp fields any longer. By invading Russia Napoleon was hoping to stop the British from receiving the Russian hemp that their navy depended on. Napoleon believed that by stopping the hemp trade the British would eventually have to cannibalize the Royal Navy and this would weaken the British naval blockade. This came less than one week after America declared war on Great Britain for impressments of American vessels and sailors, the violation of neutral rights, and the refusal to withdraw from forts along the Canadian frontier.

Within seven days JQA's home country had gone to war with England and he was living in a country being invaded by Napoleon. This next section will reveal how the hemp trade was at the root of both wars and how American merchants played middlemen in financing Russia's army. Many of the details recorded in this account came directly from JQA's personal letters and was compiled by Alfred W. Crosby in his 1965 book *America, Russia, Hemp and Napoleon.* I urge my readers to pick up a copy of Crosby's book if they would like a more thorough analysis of this history.

Calm Before War

As JQA overlooked Kronstadt harbor during the first spring days of 1810 he knew he was expected to increase trade between America and Russia and he did not intend to fail.

The early years of trade between Russia and the colonies was considered a roundabout exchange. Colonists would harvest and sell tobacco to the British, who would then turn around and sell it to the Russians. The British would benefit from being the middlemen of this trade throughout the 17th and the 18th century. The early American traders focused on the successful tobacco trade, but during the early 18th century Englishmen with the knowhow to grow tobacco arrived in Russia. By the mid point of the 1700s Russian imports of tobacco had nose-dived and Russia actually began exporting large amounts of tobacco to all of Europe.

As the need for colonial tobacco disappeared shipping merchants on the eastern seaboard began supplementing tobacco with commodities picked up in the West Indies. These commodities included indigo, rice, spices and oils. Russia's elite also began purchasing large quantities of North American animal skins to meet the demands of their lavish lifestyles. The ship merchants would set sail from the Caribbean in route to an English port and would return to America carrying hemp sailcloth and cordage from Russia.

During the early years of America our farmers raised less than 1% of the hemp used for sailing, cordage, and textiles. Needless to say, the United States was completely dependent on the Russian trade. Each American vessel in the navy needed between 50-100 tons of hemp sail and cordage replaced every 2-3 years.

Due to Russia's unique way of separating the hemp fiber from the stalk, the Russians created the strongest and most durable hemp on the market. Hemp farmers in Kentucky meanwhile struggled with the manufacturing and retting of hemp. Russian farmers practiced submerging hemp stalks in ponds of standing water to separate the fiber, while Kentuckians and other hemp farmers in North America specialized in dew-retting. Dew retting was an easier method, as farmers only had to spread the hemp stalks on the field for a few weeks and let the rain and dew separate the fibers. The fiber quality that this method produced was deemed inferior to the Russian hemp and the navy refused to use the Kentucky harvested hemp. The Russian method of water-retting hemp was an extremely long process and the majority of the hemp sold at market was harvested over two years prior. I will discuss the Kentucky hemp industry in the next section.

The Russian economy during the turn of the 19th century and the decade leading up to the war of 1812 showed massive trade balances favoring Russia. The British purchased over half of all total goods exported, with the majority of the hemp supplies being used for naval stores. It was this trade relationship between Russia and Britain that kept the two European powerhouses from declaring war on each other. Britain knew that they couldn't survive without the Russian hemp manufactures and Russian bourgeoisie enjoyed the constant supply of gold that allowed the nobles to continue their life of luxury.

Even though the British remained Russia's favorite buyer, the United States soon became their second favorite. In 1803 American ships purchased 11,390,712 pounds of hemp goods, while the British purchased a whopping 47,445,362 pounds. As stated earlier a large portion of the hemp goods purchased by the British would eventually find its way onto American shores. The combined purchase total for the rest of the world's nations was only 8,639,968 pounds.[14]

During JQA's first year at St. Petersburg the number of American ships that came to Russia seeking hemp and iron exceeded the amount of Russian ships that arrived at their own port. The reason for the increase in trade was due to the on going wars in Europe. Merchant ships of warring countries would be turned into naval vessels and thus many countries depended on the Americans to bring goods across the Atlantic. Between the years of 1792 and 1807 the overall shipping by American ships went from $564 million to $1,268 million. This increase in trade created the first economic boom in America.[15] Consequently, the only Americans getting rich were the northeastern sailing merchants. Western states did not enjoy this same growth and prosperity.

To better understand the economic wars that revolved around the hemp industry, it is best to start from the beginning. It all started during the early years of the French Revolution (1789-99) when the British began confiscating American vessels going toward French ports. If it weren't for the leadership coming from the Washington administration on remaining neutral, the United States would have most likely waged war with the British. Instead, John Jay was sent to Britain in hopes of negotiating a peace treaty. The treaty was signed on November 19, 1794 and the only positive thing it did was postpone war between the two nations. Jay refused to even bring up the topic of impressments of American sailors and the Americans were forced into not trading naval stores or timber with France. After the treaty, the French felt betrayed and the Jeffersonian party was outraged for having lost a political battle to Alexander Hamilton and the Federalists. France was so outraged by this agreement that orders were given to seize any American ships on the open seas. During the first year of this policy the

French were able to commandeer over 300 American merchant ships. A horror story of the French privateers was published in the Boston Columbian Centinel on September 25, 1799. It reported that an American ship and crew had been seized and that they had brutally beat the captain before another America ship took the ship back. [16]

As the Quasi-war progressed American merchants started to realize the best way to get the respect of warring nations was by pointing the barrel right back at them. Cannons were brought onto many of the American ships and sailors armed themselves with as much firepower as they could pack. American sailors also began sailing in packs to deter would be privateers. These ocean skirmishes affected the number of ships getting to Russian ports and consequently the amount of hemp reaching America. In 1800 the semi-war with French ships ended with the signing of the Treaty of Morfontaine.

As the French gave up their efforts of seizing neutral ships, the British navy expanded their grasp on the waterways and in 1800 they had a quarrel with a Danish merchant in the Baltic. This bloody event helped convince Paul I (Czar before Alexander I) of Russia to side with Napoleon and the French over the British. As a result of the British attack the atmosphere changed in the Baltic region and trade was drastically weakened. The Russians seized all British property in their port cities and they also made it clear to everyone that there would be no trade with the British until they recognized Russia as sole owner of the island of Malta in the Mediterranean. The conflict between Russia and Great Britain created a scarcity of hemp coming from Russia and helped push more American farmers into the hemp industry. To top it all off, Paul's new foreign policy angered many of his nobles and fellow aristocrats since the flow of money coming in from the hemp and iron trade came to a sudden halt.

America wasn't the only country feeling the loss of the Russian hemp trade. The British started offering American ship captains huge sums of money to brave the Baltic and travel to Russian shores. Their mission was to buy hemp naval goods and transport them back to British ports. If the British didn't receive hemp supplies soon they would have to start cannibalizing their merchant ships in order to have enough hemp sail and cordage for their warships.

Luckily for Great Britain and the United States on March 24, Paul I of Russia died from an apparent stroke, or at least that's what was reported. In reality, the anti-British ideology around Paul had created immense anger from the nobles and the merchants who had benefited from neutral trade with the British. In the middle of the night members of Paul's inner circle broke into his room and beat him to death. The murder of Paul left his son, Alexander I in charge and he immediately withdrew from the League of Neutrality. Trade between the British and Russians was thriving once again.

About a year after the death of Paul, the British and French made peace in March of 1802, only to start warring again in May of 1803. Once again the United States was approached to help facilitate trade. During wartime Americans would tend to trade with ports as far away from the battlefields as possible. As a result St. Petersburg and Kronstadt harbor became a preferred destination for American merchants. In 1803 a record amount of hemp and iron was loaded onto American ships at Kronstadt. The Russo-American hemp trade increased so much that President Jefferson and Alexander began throwing dinners and balls on behalf of each other. President Jefferson even went as far as sending Alexander books about America's constitution.

The war between Britain and France escalated into economic warfare after the years of 1805 and 1806. Napoleon was conquering the European continent and Great Britain had devastated the majority of Napoleons naval fleet. Economic warfare meant a revision of neutral ships right's and a return to the confiscation of American ships.

The Orders in Council issued by Britain in 1807 prohibited any neutral ship to trade with any country allied with France. In return Napoleon issued the Continental System, which forced all allies to halt trade with Great Britain. With the passing of these two policies it was nearly impossible for any American ship to make it to the Russian coast. In reaction to the foreign policies of the two warring countries President Jefferson issued the Embargo Act on December 22, 1807. This act halted trade with both Britain and France in hopes of making both countries realize just how important the American merchant ships were to both economies. Jefferson's plan was not only unconstitutional, but ended up being an epic failure and hurting American merchants the most. Since Jefferson's blunder, unconstitutional laws and epic failures have gone hand in hand in American history.

Also happening in 1807 was the agreement between Napoleon and Alexander I to cease war immediately. The two leaders met on a raft in the middle of the Niemen River and it has been reported that the first thing Alexander said to Napoleon was "Sire, I hate the British as much as you do." In reply Napoleon announced, "peace is made."[17] The biggest promise of the agreement was that Alexander noted all trade with the British would be halted and the Russians were now

Napoleon's new secret agents in recruiting neutrals to wage war against the British. After a second bloody attack by the British on Denmark's neutral city of Copenhagen, Russia had seen enough and declared war on Great Britain again. By getting Russia to declare war on Great Britain, Napoleon had successfully brought Great Britain's closest trading partner (hemp supplier) under France's powerful Continental System (Napoleon's strategy to stop countries from trading with the British). The British would have to find another way to supply their Royal Navy with hemp. Between 1807 and 1808 British hemp imports dropped 65%.[18] Britain scrambled to begin growing more hemp in India, but had little success. Due to the decrease in imports and rising demand the price for hemp skyrocketed.

The increasing hemp prices were enticing to many of the American shipping merchants. Even though the Embargo Act was still in place, many of the merchants of the northeast did not respect the White House's policy. Consequently, many ships would sneak out at night to reap the benefits of supplying cheap hemp to a sellers market. Once free from America these ships could not bring goods back to the states in fear of being prosecuted, therefore, many merchants found it lucrative to act as agents for the British hemp trade. Leading up to the war of 1812 it has been reported a large portion of American ships arriving in the Baltic were actually purchasing on Britain's behalf. To go along with paying American sailors in gold to purchase hemp on their behalf, the British were also forging documents and sailing under the disguise of neutral ships, including the stars and stripes. A United States console claimed in a letter to William Pinkney on July 22, 1808, "in a short time the seas will be entirely covered with them (British ships flying the American flag) to the great detriment of the honest and fair American trader, as it is not to be expected that the Russians, Danes, and Prussians who very vigorously carry their decrees against England into execution can be long blind to this nefarious practice, and the papers being in many instances so like as with difficulty to be known from the real, the consequence will be that every ship sailing under the flag of the United States will be seized and condemned indiscriminately."[19] If not for these hemp smugglers and the convoy provided by the Royal Navy, Napoleon's Continental System would have been highly effective.

In 1809 the United States elected James Madison to succeed Jefferson and along with this change in administrations came a change in British foreign policy. Madison and King George III brought about a renewal of trading rights for the American merchants. Under the new agreement, which was finalized in late spring, American ships were granted the right to sail under the protection of the Royal Navy as long as their ships were bound for ports in northeast Europe. When the American ships finally found there way to the Russian coast they would be pleased to see plenty of hemp sail and cordage for sale. During the next few years prices would be dramatically higher and hemp prices rocketed up 80%. This increase in price allowed the first American merchants to reap large profits on their return trip to America.

Even under the protection of the Royal Navy and the huge economic incentive for captains in 1809, very few American ships made it all the way to Russia's shores. The reason behind the slow increase in shipping lay in the hands of the Danish privateers. Denmark, who had allied with Napoleon found it in their best interests to capture the neutral Americans. In 1809 Denmark seized an astonishing 61

American ships.[20] This statistic alone shows that the British were not the only violent aggressors on the sea.

These reports deeply angered the eastern shipping merchants who saw their profits get slashed by the loss of shipping vessels. The merchants pushed for war with France over Britain for this reason (Danes were allied with France). In reality, the Danes seizure of American ships involved with the Russian hemp trade had just as much of an affect on American merchants as the seizure of ships by the British and the French. In fact it wasn't until the years of 1811 and 1812 that French privateers became a realistic threat to American hemp traders.

Even if an American merchant made it all the way to the Russian coast they weren't guaranteed admission into the ports. Alexander was still trying to abide by Napoleon's Continental System and demanded the proper documentation from each ship. Traders who failed to show evidence of the ships history were either turned away or confiscated. The problem that Alexander had enforcing the Continental System lay with the Russian traders who deliberately undermined the enforcement when giving the incentive of economic gain. In other words, money talks and it was no secret in the Russian ports that the British were illegally trading with the Russians through American middlemen and false documentation. In 1809 Great Britain received double the amount of hemp products when compared to the previous year.[21]

When John Quincy Adams arrived in St. Petersburg his first duty was sorting through American papers to decipher the legit American documents from the forged British documents. In 1810, 133 American ships sailed through the

Baltic and the majority of them sailed under British protection and/or British licenses. Without JQA's expertise American merchants would of had no protection from the rule of Alexander I. JQA's also requested that Alexander ask the Danes to release any American ships that were not proven guilty of trading with Great Britain. As the fall approached in 1810 JQA became more and more outspoken toward the Continental System and pushed Russia to demand their independence from Napoleon's control.

As time wore on, JQA slowly started to win traction with Alexander and more ships started arriving in Russian ports. The increase of Russian hemp coming back to American shores pushed down prices from $435 a ton to $300 a ton.[22] This result deeply upset Henry Clay and the Kentucky hemp farmers that wanted all Americans to purchase inferior hemp from Kentucky. The trade with Russia once again brought riches to the New England states and hurt the hemp farmers in the west by driving down prices. This divided the nation even further leading up to war of 1812.

Meanwhile, Napoleon was growing frustrated with Alexander as he had good information that Russian goods were being smuggled into England via American ships. If it weren't for this illegal smuggling by Americans, Napoleon's Continental System would have been successful at cannibalizing the Royal Navy within months. Even with Napoleon's threats of war with Russia, Alexander continually persisted that his ports had claimed 96 American ships in 1810 and he would not ruin the American trade that his merchants needed to prosper.[23] If you recall the previous leader of Russia, Alexander's father had been murdered for cutting off trade with the British. Alexander new it would be foolish to cut off their gold supply again. The Russians brought up JQA's great integrity on multiple occasions in defense of Napoleon's claims that Russia was breaking the Continental System. JQA had rejected dozens of American ships with suspicion of British dealings. Alexander eventually accused Napoleon of hypocrisy, as he himself traded with Americans when it was beneficial. From the Russian's point of view Napoleon and France were trying to establish a monopoly for colonial goods. Near the end of 1810 Alexander's relationship with the French had broken-down so much that war was now evident between the two countries.

The American merchants best bet to turn a profit in the year leading up to the war of 1812 was sailing on behalf of the British. This agreement of trade became extremely lucrative, but is not discussed much in history books since there is very little documentation of the said trade. American captains would often have verbal agreements between the British to avoid documentation, as documentation would be proof of conspiring with the British. The money flowing into Russia from the British via American ships was thus used to help finance Alexander's war with Napoleon in 1812.

As Russia moved to war with Napoleon, the French confiscation of American ships skyrocketed. Before the invasion of Russia Napoleon did little to disrupt the Russo-American trade in fear it would push Russia away from the Continental System. With nothing to loose the order was given to capture all American merchant ships. Northeasterners accused the government of ignoring France's wrong doings and blowing English threats out of proportion. To go along with the French seizure of ships, the Danes, which were under Napoleon's control also brought thirty-seven American ships into their ports.[24] JQA would later demand American warships be issued to the Baltic to protect the rights of neutral shipping from the French and Danish privateers, not the British.

With Napoleon's invasion of Russia came the reopening of trade between Russian merchants and the British. That year the British hemp importation actually hit a five-year high. Just like today, during the early 19th century good business made good allies.

By the start of 1812 the War Hawks in congress were in full force. Led by hemp farmer and politician Henry Clay, the group spearheaded the war cry against Great Britain for not respecting neutral shipping rights. Meanwhile, the Americans on the Northeast coast (ship owners) were pushing for peace with the British and war with the French. In reality, we know that the British were not the only country seizing American ships (France and Denmark were feared more by American captains) and many of the American ships were being aided to Russia in a British convey or even working directly under the British in illegal trade schemes.

Not wanting to go to war with America the British decided on June 16, 1812 to revoke the Orders in Council when dealing with American traders. Two days later James Madison, unknowing of the British change of policy declared war on Great Britain. Consequently, James Madison had not only declared war on the British, but also declared war during the heart of the shipping season and with a large portion of American ships trapped on the European coastline. Why would the President make such a big error and endanger his citizens?

John Quincy Adams was furious about the war declaration since he realized it would jeopardize any Russo-American hemp trade that still existed. Adams agreed with the northeastern states and believed there was not a legitimate reason to go to war with the British, especially since they had restored American rights two days before the war declaration. Adams like many American merchants wanted peace to be restored immediately and trade to resume. JQA was also a member of Madison's political party so this disagreement did not lie just between party boundaries. The disgruntled and trapped American sailors instantly started looking for ways back to America and many of them approached the British for help. Those American captains who held British trading licenses were granted passage to Great Britain under the protection of the Royal Navy. Once they deposited their hemp and iron at a British port they were allowed to travel back to America.

In December of 1814 John Quincy Adams, along with other American politicians managed to negotiate a peace treaty with the British and the hemp economic war of 1812 was brought to a halt. Even with the end of the war the Russo-American hemp trade would never take off quite like it did in the years leading up to the war.

In the end hemp proved to be just as important to the men and women of the 16th, 17th, 18th and 19th century as oil is to the developed nations of today. Wars have been fought over control of the hemp trade and wars have and will continually be fought over the control of oil. The answer lays in finding alternatives to fossil fuels. Could hemp hold the answer?

Kentucky Hemp History

During the years following World War I and continuing for the majority of the 20th century, Kentucky's most famous and profitable cash crop has been tobacco. Tobacco has also been the most deadly crop cultivated during this time. In recent years the profitability of this crop has declined and farmers in Kentucky have been looking for answers on how to keep their family farms afloat. Many farmers are now looking to their past to find the answer.

Outside of historian and farming circles, many people have no idea that during the 19th century the bluegrass region of Kentucky was the nations leading producer of industrial hemp. During the last years of the hemp boom it is estimated that Kentucky produced 94 percent of the entire national hemp crop and 90 percent of the Kentucky crop was grown within the bluegrass region of the state.[25] Many of the farmers in this area are now asking themselves; why can't we have opportunity to make a living growing industrial hemp like our fathers and grandparents did?

The birth of the state and the development of the hemp fields of Kentucky go hand in hand. James F. Hopkins wrote the most thorough documentation of Kentucky's hemp industry in 1951 called the *History Of The Hemp Industry In Kentucky*. Much of the information I will be writing about in this section was gathered from Hopkin's work.

As the eastern seaboard began increasing in population more and more people felt the need to move west to secure land and a better future for themselves. The West was an unforgiving area however and Native American attacks on the first settlers were common. Consequently, the first hemp crops were grown right outside military settlements. The first man credited with sowing hemp seeds was Archibald McNeil in 1775 near Clark's Creek, right outside of Danville Kentucky.[26]

During the same year that McNeil planted his hemp crop Daniel Boone was busy creating the Wilderness Road. The Wilderness Road would allow thousands of settlers to make their way into the Kentucky bluegrass region. As more people arrived farms started spreading further away from forts and hemp seeds were in high demand. Once harvested, hemp fiber was originally processed in homes using spinning wheels and small hand looms. The fiber would be woven into rope, bagging, and clothing for the settlers.

After the states won their independence from the British, the flood of settlers became more profound than ever and the fiber from hemp was needed to keep up with the high demand for textiles. Hemp along with other frontier goods would eventually be used for bartering. As more hemp fields started popping up, small manufactures started establishing themselves to purchase large quantities of hemp fiber and oil. The major hemp weaving businesses were called "ropewalks" and they started to attract more investments during the 1790s.

Many Kentuckians and avid bourbon drinkers associate the name Elijah Craig with being one of the best bourbon makers in the world, but in 1793 Elijah established one of the first ropewalks in Kentucky.[27] A few years later in 1798 Elijah would open up his second ropewalk on the fertile banks of the Kentucky River.

One of the biggest problems farmers had after harvesting their hemp was getting their products to market. Shipping their goods over the Appalachian Mountains was too expensive and the only other option was floating their hemp downstream to New Orleans on flat boats. This proved to be difficult at times since the Spanish had control of New Orleans and were found to be unreliable trading partners. One of the first big developments in regards to free trade occurred in 1795 when the Pinckney Treaty was signed. This guaranteed the rights to trade on the Mississippi and ushered in the era of the Mississippi boatmen.

Accompanying the free trade from New Orleans came a gradual rise in the standard of living in Kentucky. Opening up free trade then and now creates prosperity for all parties involved. Kentucky farmers began reaping larger profits and shipping merchants along the Ohio River became popular middlemen in the Kentucky hemp trade. During the first half of 1801 the Port of Louisville recorded shipping "42,048 pounds of hemp and 2,402 hundredweight, 73 pounds of cable and storage."[28] Prosperity was short lived however and Spain would shut down trade on multiple occasions.

To add to the hardships of trading with the unreliable Spanish, western farmers and manufacturers also had to deal with an increase in international competition. A break between the warring countries of Europe during this time allowed cheap foreign goods to flow into the country. The result of this influx of foreign goods was a drop in commodity prices throughout the country. The cheaper and far more superior Russian hemp hit the Kentucky industry hard and the demand for protective tariffs thus began in the manufacturing areas and especially in the Western states. Thomas Wallace became one of the first citizens to demand protection for hemp and hemp products, "adequate to prevent or lessen the importation of them, and to give encouragement to the husbandmen and manufacturers of our own country."[29]

During this time the biggest market for hemp products was the cotton industry that was aided by the invention of the cotton gin. The increase in supply of cotton caused an increase in the need for bagging materials that could be made from Kentucky hemp. By the end of the first decade of the 19th century Kentuckians supplied the majority of the southern cotton farmers with cordage, rope, and bagging.

Hemp fiber was not the only raw material in high demand; hemp entrepreneurs also demanded hemp and flax seed. George Leibe's oil mill was located on Limestone road in Lexington where he made oil out of the seeds. Henry Clay was also involved in the first hemp corporations in 1808.[30]

In 1809 Kentuckians again lobbied congress for a more effective duty on hemp, yet only to have the request rejected. By 1810 Kentucky was home to 38 ropewalks that produced nearly 2,000 tons of hemp cordage. A year later it was estimated that around 60 ropewalks were producing hemp cordage.[31]

Although Kentucky had their hemp duty request rejected, many believed that hemp farmers would benefit from the War of 1812. Kentucky congressmen and hemp farmer Henry Clay found himself leading the efforts in congress to wage war with Great Britain. On March 14, 1812 Clay wrote to his followers about the upcoming war, "The effect of doubling the existing duties, will be to subject foreign hemp to a duty of 40 dollars per ton, instead of 20, which it now pays. In the event of war, I am inclined to think that article will command a better price than it now does."[32] Clay was successful in his efforts to go to war with the British, but his prediction of a prosperous hemp market came up short. By 1813 the prices for hemp had barely risen. This did not stop the boom in the hemp industry however, The Niles Register, a reliable publication at the time stated in 1814 that the amount of ropewalks in the state of Kentucky had increased 100% since 1810.

After the war of 1812 foreign hemp and other goods once again flooded America's ports with cheap & superior products. The British had a surplus of supplies that were built up from wartime and were now unloading these goods at low prices. This however had little affect on the Kentucky hemp industry since the foreign hemp would only be purchased by the shipping industry and was not needed for bagging cotton. The American Navy favored the Russian hemp because of the way it was processed and submerged under water to separate the fibers as opposed to the way Kentuckians just dew-retted their hemp. As a result of the cheap foreign goods, the Tariff of 1816 was passed levying a duty of $30 per ton on imported hemp, along with a 25% tariff on cotton, woolen textiles, and iron.[33] Many Kentucky hemp farmers were holding out hope that the shipping industry would eventually start buying Kentucky hemp due to the high tariff. Southerners were wary to jump on board with the tariff, but in the end, both protectionist and free market thinkers realized that the government needed revenue to pay for the war and it was either going to come from tariffs or excise taxes. In the end the Southerners sided with the west and the northeast since the tariff was only suppose to be temporary. Much of the south was also experiencing tremendous economic success and they did not believe the tariff would be much of an issue.

After the War of 1812 the cotton industry increased their exports and the demand for cheap hemp bailing materials increased. An agriculture group called the Kentucky Society even offered a silver cup to the manufacturer who produced the best hemp or flax linen.[34] The rise in prices gave farmers the incentive to grow more hemp, which would eventually cause an oversupply and a consequential drop in prices leading up to the Panic of 1819.

The Panic of 1819 was the first major economic recession in America and many of the smaller hemp manufacturers had to shut their doors. Kentucky was one of the hardest hit states during the panic since the textile factories that wove hemp into fabrics had experienced one of the biggest booms during the years leading up to the Panic. The Panic of 1819 was caused by an expansion of the money supply that can trace its roots back to the war of 1812. The problem was compounded in 1817 when the Second Bank of the United States was founded in order to slow inflation and the credit expansion. Instead of accomplishing its goal the bank was only successful at creating more credit and cheap money. The expansion of the money supply caused businessmen to misjudge future demand and by the end of the recession people were making jokes about how worthless their bank notes were due to inflation. In Kentucky a large portion of the credit expansion was used to finance the expanding hemp industry and is the reason why the hemp industry was hit hard during the panic. Kentucky and Tennessee were two states that recommended bailing out banks the most and consequently lagged behind in the recovery. States that practiced conservative banking and kept a larger percentage of gold and silver on hand to repay bank notes did much better during this crisis.

One of the few bright spots in the Kentucky economy immediately following the panic was the rebound of hemp prices. During the panic farmers cut back on the amount of acreage devoted to hemp, thus decreasing the supply and increasing the price paid. The year of 1819 saw hemp drop to $80 per ton, but by 1820 the price for hemp had gone up to $100 per ton.[35]

As stated earlier Henry Clay was a hemp farmer in Lexington Kentucky, but more importantly he was the designer of the "American System" that called for high tariffs to protect agriculture and manufacturing sectors. After the panic of 1819 many citizens and politicians wrongly blamed the market for the depression as opposed to the bank credit expansion and many felt it necessary to support high tariffs. The protective tariffs incorporated into Clay's American System would then help fund the improvements of roads and canals. The American System was considered one of the first centralized plans in the United States and was engineered to benefit the west, northern manufacturers, and the Kentucky hemp farmer. Due to the American System's mercantilist policies it was deemed unconstitutional by a handful of presidents. Even though Clay found many followers in Kentucky by preaching his protective tariff it would eventually become one of the main factors why Lincoln did not want the South to secede. Many historians argue that this was the main economic force that led to the civil war. If the south were to peacefully succeed foreign countries would be more inclined to trade with the south as opposed to the North. Clay and the tariff issue got the majority of their support due to the poor economic times and the cries from citizens for legislative action during times of crisis.

As westerners argued for increase in protection, the southern states passionately argued against the increase. Politicians who were against the protective tariffs argued that foreign countries would not import as many American exports since there would be less American dollars circulating in foreigner's hands. Opponents of the tariff also cited retaliation tariffs that would be proposed by trading partners. Both of these scenarios would thus be a net loss to the overall economy. Southerners who supported the Tariff of 1816 because of war debts and patriotism for American business were not so thrilled by the extension and increased tariffs. This re-distribution of wealth from the south to manufacturing in the north & west was not to be tolerated. The south was most upset by the tariff since they depended on exporting agricultural goods and importing the majority of their manufactured goods. With the new tariff laws the south was forced to purchase overpriced and inferior goods from northern manufacturers. Henry Clay would end up winning the majority of these tariff battles at the expense of the south and to the benefit of northern manufacturers, westerners, and most of all the Kentucky hemp farmers. While Kentucky merchants won, everyone else was paying higher prices and/or using lower quality hemp. The hemp suppliers benefited from these mercantilist policies at the expense of the South, but hemp would not be so lucky during the 1930s.

The heated tariff debate that started in 1816 and divided the nation in 1820 would set the political tone for the next 40 years. In 1824 a new tariff bill was passed that increased the tax on iron, lead, wool, hemp and cotton bagging.[36] The increased duty on hemp once again had little effect on the hemp trade since ship builders would still not purchase the inferior Kentucky grown hemp. Instead of spurring on growth in the American hemp market, the tariff was only successful in causing the ship building industry to decline. The tariff on cotton bagging however had a direct impact on the amount of hemp bagging demanded by southern cotton farmers. The raw cotton material had to be bagged before shipping and the tariff of 1824 forced all southern planters to purchase the hemp bagging from Kentucky as opposed to the cheap bagging from overseas. As you can see the tariff was simply a redistribution of wealth from the South to the Midwest. The Kentucky hemp farmers benefited, but the ship building industry was a victim and the cotton farmers in the south were forced to incur higher expenses in the form of hemp bagging. A representative of the cotton industry claimed that the hemp bagging from Kentucky was so poor that many planters preferred paying the tariff than using the domestic bagging. After passing of the tariff, Kentuckian, Nathaniel Hart declared "Hemp is the only article in Kentucky in demand, (except our livestock), and this in consequence of the protecting duty it has received."[37] Political party affiliation did not matter during the year 1824 as all northern and western leaders voiced the importance of the protective tariff.

In the South it was well known that Henry Clay was the leader behind the hemp tariffs and many Southerners went out of their way to avoid Clay's hemp. Hopkins writes, "A rumor to the effect that Henry Clay was extensively engaged in manufacturing bagging was current in Virginia in 1825, and a Lexingtonian who sent two wagons loaded with baling materials to South Carolina in the previous year found difficulty in selling the shipment because of a belief that it was the vanguard of a caravan of 300 wagons bringing Clay's bale rope and bagging to a market from which competition had been excluded by Clay's tariff."[38] Clay was literally lining his pockets by pushing congress to pass mercantilist policies that protected his hemp industry. This should sound familiar to you as it is still going on today in the energy, pharmaceutical, farming, prison, banking and healthcare industries. Today politicians are simply rewarded with kickbacks and cushy jobs after they leave the public sector.

Throughout the 1820s the price for hemp remained volatile. Henry Clay wrote, "The price is not uniform. The extremes have been as low as three, and as high as eight dollars, for the long hundred-the customary mode of selling it. The most general price, during a term of many years, has been from four to five dollars. At five dollars it compensates well the labor of the grower and is considered more profitable than anything else the farmer has cultivated."[39]

In 1828 the highest hemp duty was passed in the Tariff of Abominations. In the book *Tariff History of the United States,* F.W. Taussig writes, "The most important of the proposed duties on raw materials, however, were on hemp, flax, and wool. The existing duty on hemp was $35 per ton. It was proposed to increase it immediately to $45, and further to increase it by an annual increment of $5, till it should finally reach $60."[40] The 1828 tariff also fixed cotton bagging for a year at 4.5 cents per square yard and 5 cents a square yard after the first year.

The passing of the 1828 Tariff of Abominations caused uproar in the south and almost led to a Civil War during the early 1830s. Due to the outrage coming from the south, in 1832 the duty on hemp was decreased from $60 per ton to $40.[41] One year later the Compromise Tariff would pass lowering all duties until they would reach 1816 levels. The Compromise Tariff came about after South Carolina, led by John C. Calhoun threatened secession from the Union. Threats of secession were spurred on by the nullification crisis that claimed the previous tariffs were unconstitutional in the state of South Carolina.

By the year of 1833 the price of hemp was once again falling and by the end of the summer hit $60 per ton. The hard times were short lived however and 1835 saw a bounce back in prices to $150 per ton, prosperity would continue until the Panic of 1837. Hemp would stay profitable during the economic problems that started in 1837, but the farmer had very little left after paying out expenses.[42]

Similar to the Panic of 1819, the Panic of 1837 also came about by an expansion of bank notes and easy money. In 1830 the total money supply was $109 million and by 1837 the money supply was up to $267 million.[43] This expansion in the money supply came from both the central bank and the state banks that were being run by reckless "wildcat" bankers. During the years of 1839 to 1843 the money supply contracted as banks called in loans and close to a quarter of all banks failed. Many historians have wrongly claimed that this contraction of money created deflation, which wrecked the economy. In actuality the deflation caused wholesale prices to drop 42 percent and according to a paper done by economist Joseph Salerno, "real GNP (Gross National Product) and real consumption actually increased during this period by 16 percent and 21 percent, respectively. However, real investment did decline during this period by 23 percent, which was a benign development, because the malinvestments of the previous inflationary boom needed to be liquidated."[44]

The duties agreed on in 1833 would last for nine years until Henry Clay pushed his hand again regarding protective duties for hemp. Hopkins wrote, "The decrease in protection pleased neither Clay, who drew up the act of 1833, nor many of his fellow Kentuckians; and agitation began for an increase in rates. A Great Tariff Meeting in Maysville in May, 1842, at which Adam Beatty played a leading role, adopted resolutions which reflected the protectionist philosophy."[45] The Tariff of 1842 ended up restoring hemp duties to their 1832 levels.

With the old protection levels back in place the hemp industry saw a boom in the amount of commodities being sold throughout the rest of the 1840s. Neighboring states also began taking part in the hemp trade and the Mississippi River saw a huge influx of the amount of hemp being floated downstream to New Orleans on Flat Boats.

As competition from other states continued to increase Kentuckians began looking for ways to create better products and increase their potential market. The protective tariff could not help them when competing against their fellow Americans. Many farmers began experimenting with alternative techniques in separating the hemp fiber from the stalk. As stated earlier Kentuckians dew-retted their hemp instead of submerging it under water to separate the fiber from the stalk. The Water retted hemp had a higher market price, but the work, time, and capital needed to create the dumping tanks or ponds made it difficult to try and even harder to execute. Southern cotton planters even started experimenting with new bagging material in hopes to eliminate the artificially high prices of their current hemp bagging materials. This fact pushed more and more farmers into the hemp water retting business in hopes that the US navy and other ship builders would eventually purchase their higher quality hemp supplies instead of the Russian goods. Henry Clay even began water retting a portion of his hemp fields and in 1843 he sent a shipment of his hemp to a Baltimore shipbuilding yard where it was said to be "the best American hemp that has ever appeared in this market."[46]

Even after implementing the new water-retting techniques the quality of hemp products coming from Kentucky remained poor. One southern farmer from Louisiana wrote, "I have been planting in this State for a number of years past, and I have been in the habit of uniformly purchasing Kentucky bagging and rope, until within a few years past, when I commenced purchasing East India and Scotch, in consequence of the Kentucky being so inferior. It would appear good on the outside of the roll, but, after taking off a little, it would present another quality greatly inferior. The rope generally ran the same way; the outside smooth and even, within coarse and gouty. It has always been my wish to encourage the manufactures of my own country in preference to any other: but, by being deceived so often, I had almost concluded not to purchase again from Kentucky. Many of my neighbors had come to the same conclusion."[47] Many who are against protective tariffs and corporate welfare for domestic industries believe this inferiority can be blamed on the protective nature of the industry and the lack of technological innovation on the part of the Kentucky hemp entrepreneurs. This is important to understand because once we reintroduce hemp in America, hemp farmers will not be protected with tariffs and will have to develop the industry using innovation and hard work.

Henry Clay can be looked at as the founder of the Kentucky hemp industry, but he also sowed the seeds of its demise. The mercantilist policies that Clay adopted from Alexander Hamilton would eventually be accepted by Northern Republicans and then replicated by the Democrats. You will soon learn that big business and big government would team up again to pass mercantilist policies in the 1930s. This time the hemp industry, the environment, and the public would suffer the consequences.

Chapter 2: Prohibition Theory

"One of the great mistakes is to judge policies and programs by their intentions rather than their results."- Milton Friedman

After the Civil War the hemp industry in Kentucky never fully recovered due to the lack of cheap labor, the invention of the steam engine, and competition from cotton bagging in the South. Even with these setbacks the industry pushed ahead between the years 1869 and 1889. During these two decades hemp production jumped from 155 tons to 1,000 tons in 1889.[48] After 1889 the inability to create efficient harvesting & processing equipment kept hemp in a decline until the early 1900s.

In 1916 Lyster H. Dewey attempted to revive the

industrial hemp industry and said, "Without doubt, hemp will continue to be one of the staple agricultural crops of the United States."[49] That year hemp cultivation increased due to WWI and by 1917 farmers planted around 42,000 acres.[50]

Between the years of 1880 to the early 1930s hemp recordkeeping was sketchy at best. A report by the Federal Bureau of Narcotics stated that "from 1880 to 1933 the hemp grown in the United States had declined from 15,000 to 1,200 acres, and that the price of line hemp had dropped."[51] The FBN also reported that during the 1930s they started to see a reversal in the declining trend. Multiple companies were growing industrial hemp for new contracts; in 1934 hemp was cultivated on 6,400 acres of American soil and by 1937 it had risen to 10,900 acres.[52] That's an 808% increase in the amount of hemp cultivated in 4 years! An industry that was using hemp seed oil in large quantities was the paint industry. In 1935 roughly 116 million pounds of hempseed was used just for paints and varnishes.[53]

The increase in cultivation was spurred on by a new invention that processed industrial hemp fiber more efficiently. This led to heavy speculation and renewed interest in the byproduct cellulose that could be used to make paper, cellophane, and plastics. This invention called the decorticator solved a problem that was 6,000 years old. There are many different versions of decorticators, but George Schlichten patented the first American hemp decorticator in 1919. Sadly, George died without seeing his invention in action, but a decade and a couple of modifications later investors began to take notice. This speculation led Mechanical Engineering magazine to write an article in 1937 claiming industrial hemp to be "the most profitable and desirable crop that can be grown." [54] One year later (after the Marihuana Tax Act was passed) Popular Mechanics magazine wrote hemp was the "new billion dollar crop".[55]

New Billion Dollar Crop: Popular Mechanics, February 1938

"AMERICAN farmers are promised a new cash crop with an annual value of several hundred million dollars, all because a machine has been invented which solves a problem more than 6,000 years old. It is hemp, a crop that will not compete with other American products.

Instead, it will displace imports of raw material and manufactured products produced by underpaid coolie and peasant labor and it will provide thousands of jobs for American workers throughout the land.

The machine which makes this possible is designed for removing the fiber-bearing cortex from the rest of the stalk, making hemp fiber available for use without a prohibitive amount of human labor. Hemp is the standard fiber of the world. It has great tensile strength and durability. It is used to produce more than 5,000 textile products, ranging from rope to fine laces, and the woody "hurds" remaining after the fiber has been removed contain more than seventy-seven per cent cellulose, and can be used to produce more than 25,000 products, ranging from dynamite to Cellophane.

Machines now in service in Texas, Illinois, Minnesota and other states are producing fiber at a manufacturing cost of half a cent a pound, and are finding a profitable market for the rest of the stalk. Machine operators are making a good profit in competition with coolie-produced foreign fiber while paying farmers fifteen dollars a ton for hemp as it comes from the field.

From the farmers' point of view, hemp is an easy crop to grow and will yield from three to six tons per acre on any land that will grow corn, wheat, or oats. It has a short growing season, so that it can be planted after other crops are in. It can be grown in any state of the union. The long roots penetrate and break the soil to leave it in perfect condition for the next year's crop. The dense shock of leaves, eight to twelve feet above the ground, chokes out weeds. Two successive crops are enough to reclaim land that has been abandoned because of Canadian thistles or quack grass.

Under old methods, hemp was cut and allowed to lie in the fields for weeks until it "retted" enough so the fibers could be pulled off by hand. Retting is simply rotting as a result of dew, rain and bacterial action. Machines were developed to separate the fibers mechanically after retting was complete, but the cost was high, the loss of fiber great, and the quality of fiber comparatively low.

With the new machine, known as a decorticator, hemp is cut with a slightly modified grain binder. It is delivered to the machine where an automatic chain conveyor feeds it to the breaking arms at the rate of two or three tons per hour. The hurds are broken into fine pieces which drop into the hopper, from where they are delivered by blower to a baler or to truck or freight car for loose shipment. The fiber comes from the other end of the machine, ready for baling.

From this point on almost anything can happen. The raw fiber can be used to produce strong twine or rope, woven into burlap, used for carpet warp or linoleum backing or it may be bleached and refined, with resinous by-products of high commercial value. It can, in fact, be used to replace the foreign fibers which now flood our markets.

Thousands of tons of hemp hurds are used every year by one large powder company for the manufacture of dynamite and TNT. A large paper company, which has been paying more than a million dollars a year in duties on foreign-made cigarette papers, now is manufacturing these papers from American hemp grown in Minnesota. A new factory in Illinois is producing fine bond papers from hemp. The natural materials in hemp make it an economical source of pulp for any grade of paper manufactured, and the high percentage of alpha cellulose promises an unlimited supply of raw material for the thousands of cellulose products our chemists have developed.

It is generally believed that all linen is produced from flax. Actually, the majority comes from hemp--authorities estimate that more than half of our imported linen fabrics are manufactured from hemp fiber. Another misconception is that burlap is made from hemp. Actually, its source is usually jute, and practically all of the burlap we use is woven by laborers in India who receive only four cents a day. Binder twine is usually made from sisal which comes from Yucatan and East Africa.

All of these products, now imported, can be produced from home- grown hemp. Fish nets, bow strings, canvas, strong rope, overalls, damask tablecloths, fine linen

Our imports of foreign fabrics and fibers average about $200,000,000 per year; in raw fibers alone we imported over $50,000,000 in the first six months of 1937. All of this income can be made available for Americans.

The paper industry offers even greater possibilities. As an industry it amounts to over $1,000,000,000 a year, and of that eighty per cent is imported. But hemp will produce every grade of paper, and government figures estimate that 10,000 acres devoted to hemp will produce as much paper as 40,000 acres of average pulp land.

One obstacle in the onward march of hemp is the reluctance of farmers to try new crops. The problem is complicated by the need for proper equipment a reasonable distance from the farm. The machine cannot be operated profitably unless there is enough acreage within driving range and farmers cannot find a profitable market unless there is machinery to handle the crop. Another obstacle is that the blossom of the female hemp plant contains marijuana, a narcotic, and it is impossible to grow hemp without producing the blossom. Federal regulations now being drawn up require registration of hemp growers, and tentative proposals for preventing narcotic production are rather stringent.

However, the connection of hemp as a crop and marijuana seems to be exaggerated. The drug is usually produced from wild hemp or locoweed that can be found on vacant lots and along railroad tracks in every state. If federal regulations can be drawn to protect the public without preventing the legitimate culture of hemp, this new crop can add immeasurably to American agriculture and industry."

It is important to note that most of the facts in this article were found to be true in the 1930s and may not be true today due to new research and innovation. After reading this article I hope my readers begin to understand the true potential that the hemp industry had leading up to its prohibition. The writers however, were not aware, or clearly did not fully understand the consequences of the Marihuana Tax Act that had passed the previous year.

The years leading up to the prohibition of hemp saw business cartels in both America and Europe growing more powerful with the help of corrupt politicians. Much of the world was struggling economically and many people demanded that their political leaders help fix the problems that their previous economic policies had created. This became the perfect opportunity for politicians and business leaders to pass mercantilist policies under the disguise of protecting the public. In reality these policies did not help the public and they were only successful in promoting a more "corporate run" state.

Not everyone supported the ever-growing supremacy of the business cartels and the chemical industry. Critics such as George Washington Carver, Thomas Edison, and Henry Ford were among the few who supported free markets and a decentralized farming industry. These leaders believed that the economic policies that were being passed by government and being forced onto businesses would not only eliminate competition and slow innovation, but it would be successful in giving more power to the elite ruling class. Considering that the Great Depression was twice as long as any economic downturn in recent times I would say the critics were dead on.

As more farmers and processors became interested in the hemp industry, legislation in congress was quickly being fashioned to halt the growing market. The Marihuana Tax Act of 1937 (MTA) surprisingly caught hemp farmers off guard since lawmakers only expressed interest in stopping African Americans and Mexicans from smoking marihuana. Even though the bill was fashioned to only target drug users, it ended up creating a large grey area between hemp and marijuana. Hemp was not outlawed by the MTA, but hemp farmers and processors were put at a disadvantage due to the new taxes on their industry.

To ensure the hemp farmers that all was well, the Federal Bureau of Narcotics Commissioner Harry Anslinger pledged that the legislation would not have any negative effect on the hemp industry. However, shortly after the passing of the MTA, Mr. Anslinger made his intentions more noticeable when he established penalties (taxes) for violating the act and included the possession of hemp stalks that had to many leaves. Due to the law the farmers could not transport their hemp crops without removing the majority of the hemp leaves that resembled marijuana leaves. This was completely inefficient and unnecessary as there was no proper way to remove all leaves except by allowing the crop to naturally dew rot. Unfortunately, the farmers were left at the mercy of mother earth and how many leaves the winds and rains were able to knock off the stalk.

Ironically in 1937, DuPont Corporation was given a patent for the processes of making plastics from oil and coal. In their annual report to stockholders DuPont Company recommend investors to make bold investments in their new petrochemical division. This new patent process allowed DuPont to produce synthetics such as nylon (replaced hemp canvas), rayon, plastics, cellophane and methanol. If hemp would have been allowed to compete with these chemical companies in a free market it would of gotten the support of rural communities everywhere and thus a large share of DuPont's profits. Hemp also would have lessened the environmental strain that these companies manufacturer on a daily basis. DuPont's chemical patents and processes combined with government subsidies also made it beneficial and cheaper to produce paper from wood pulp. This gave landowners that were looking to profit off their tree pulp the incentive to lobby congress for mercantilist policies that prohibited a competitive hemp industry.

Along with DuPont's involvement in America they also struck a major deal with I.G. Farben In 1929. I.G. Farben was a chemical and drug-producing powerhouse in Hitler's Germany and was the most prominent business cartel in the world. I.G had major deals with over 2,000 companies and it included many companies that are still traded on Wall Street. DuPont was I.G Farben's biggest American competitor and in the past had walked away from deals with I.G on the account that I.G wanted to become the dominant player in the deal. After the Rockefellers and their oil corporations struck a deal with the I.G. cartel, DuPont realized it must jump on board or risk tremendous domestic competition from Standard Oil (New Jersey) and its subsidiaries. An investigation regarding I.G. Farben's partnership with Standard and DuPont began in 1941, but was quickly dropped during the war because all parties involved were needed for war materials. It is important to note that I.G. Farben was the chemical supplier for all of the Holocaust gas chambers (Zyklon B) and the company was disassembled after World War II because of war crimes. Due to the mercantilist policies set up by business cartels and government intervention I.G. Farben and its partners were the largest profiteers from World War II.[56]

This business cartel would not of existed if it wasn't for the help of successful politicians on both sides of the Atlantic. The cartel was established in over 90 countries and included both banks and businesses. In essence it became the official puppet master of every influential politician and intellectual.

The prohibition theory surrounding industrial hemp and the DuPont Corporation involves a vast array of high profile businessmen and governmental figures. Andrew Mellon, who was DuPont's banker and Secretary of the U.S. Treasury was the inside man and his friend and media mogul William Randolph Hearst molded public opinion. While DuPont was securing chemical patent rights, Hearst, the owner of the most established newspaper chain in the U.S. was focused on his vast acreage of timberland and was investing in paper mills to manufacture newspaper using DuPont's chemicals.

In order to successfully prohibit the new competition from industrial hemp, Mellon and the business cartel realized that they must vilify marijuana and make sure hemp was included. In order to accomplish this Mellon constructed a new government agency to regulate drugs and called it the Federal Bureau of Narcotics. Mellon would choose Harry Anslinger to head the new multimillion-dollar agency. The purpose of this agency would be to make a public issue out of marijuana, degrade minorities, and employ the men who had lost their jobs after alcohol prohibition. On the outside it only looked like this agency was targeting minorities, but Mellon's real agenda was to slow and eventually eradicate hemp farmers as a competitor to his business cartel.

Mellon was worried that the hemp breakthroughs that occurred during the previous years were a direct threat on his and his friends businesses. His two biggest fans Randolph Hearst with his wood paper industry and Lammont Dupont with his petrochemical production would reap the benefits of hemp prohibition at the expense of the consumers and the environment. Mellon would also benefit from owning stock of the companies that were poised to increase market share.

The discovery of hemp bio-diesel, which was published in Popular Mechanics in 1937, gave oil companies another reason to lobby for the prohibition of hemp. Needless to say they were not sad to see hemp suffer as a result of the MTA. Oil companies were also stressing about reports claiming that the hemp plant could produce the same high quality plastics without using petroleum. The studies at the time showed that this new hemp plastic was lighter and stronger than steel! Henry Ford himself was one of the leaders in crafting plastics out of biomass.

Gulf Oil was one of the seven major players in the oil industry (cartel) and Andrew Mellon of all people was their Ambassador to London. It is estimated that the Mellon family owned around a quarter of the Gulf shares according to Anthony Sampson's book, "The Seven Sisters". Talk about a conflict of interest. During this same decade pharmaceutical companies (owned by the same oil & chemical cartels) started producing mass quantities of synthetic drugs that would replace herbal medicines. For thousands of years certain cannabis sativa strains were used to treat multiple diseases and illnesses.

DuPont showed their involvement in the passage of the Marihuana Act of 1937 when in that years report to stockholders they urged investors to continue to invest in their synthetic product opportunities. Their reasoning was that they were expecting changes in the "revenue raising power of government converted into an instrument for forcing acceptance of sudden new ideas of industrial and social reorganization."[57] This new revenue would be coming after the interest in the hemp industry was eradicated from the market. People must understand that the cartels number one reason for being in business was to eliminate all potential competition on the free market.

"Competition is sin" – John D. Rockefeller

Eventually law enforcement started singling out immigrants, sexual deviants and misfits who listened to jazz music. After Harry Anslinger took his new position at The Federal Bureau of Narcotics, his first task was to investigate reports that immigrants from Mexico were smoking chronic buds from the flowers of the hemp plant. At this point in American history racism toward immigrants, people of color and especially Mexicans was at a high. President FDR even snubbed 4-time Olympic gold medalist and African American Jessie Owens after the 1936 games. Owens said, "Hitler didn't snub me – it was FDR that snubbed me."[58] Many stories have been passed along saying that Hitler refused to acknowledge Owens, but Owens recognized that Hitler gave him more respect by shaking his hand off stage than his own president. This racism that was showcased by our highest public office was even worse in the media outlets. Stories were fabricated about how colored people get aggressive and violent after smoking marijuana. Anslinger also started referring to hemp as marihuana, the slang word for the plant that was smoked by Mexicans. This was the first time hemp was labeled marijuana in the public's eye. Hearst's papers were quick to demonize Mexicans as he was in a constant struggle for land rights in Mexico due to Apache resistance.

The majority of the population shaped their views from reading Hearst's media and sadly he influenced an entire generation with his lies. Hemp was demonized in every possible way based on one-sided horror stories. Consequently these stories never mentioned the true benefits of industrial hemp and its vast array of uses. Yellow journalism had been a problem with Hearst media distributions since the late 19th century and the yellow journalism promoted by Hearst against hemp has to be one of the most notorious cases. Unfortunately people from all over the world still fall into the trap of listening to the talking heads on TV without doing their own research.

With marijuana fever taking over the media outlets and the national opinion, Harry Anslinger took his case to the US Congress. Leading up to debates regarding the Marijuana Tax Act of 1937, Anslinger chose not to bring up to the committee that marijuana was the same thing as hemp. Supporters of industrial hemp and the hemp farmers discovered this omission of facts nearly to late. Only after hearing testimony from the hemp industry did they decide to modify the wording of the bill to allow for the continued farming of industrial hemp. Even though hemp was still grown, future investors became weary of the industry due to the added regulations, taxes and mercantilist policies (government subsidies) that gave incentives to hemp's competitors. The result was the development of economies where a select group of individuals and businesses control a vast majority of the wealth.

Learning about how hemp became regulated and taxed is only half the story. To better understand how the hemp industry disappeared one really has to pay attention to the corporate subsidies that were being handed to hemp's competitors. Due to the government's take over of agriculture farmers were given the incentive to grow corn, soybeans, and cotton instead of hemp. The government had guaranteed prices of hemp's competition and farmers that grew hemp would be throwing guaranteed money away. The chemical industry also began receiving government subsidies during the 1930s at the expense of the hemp industry. These subsidies were in the form of tax breaks, military protection, and externalities.

Although Anslinger promised that the hemp industry would not suffer, lawmakers knew very well that the power to tax was the power to prohibit. On March 29, 1937 the

Supreme Court upheld a law that deterred gun use by taxing machine guns. With the rubber stamp approval from the Supreme Court, this legislation paved the way for the Marihuana Tax Act. If it was constitutional to prohibit machine guns through taxation, it was also constitutional to prohibit the cultivation of hemp through taxation. Lawmaker's purpose in passing the tax act was not to raise revenue, but to prohibit hemp from being grown. Anslinger claimed the legislation was only enacted to regulate the usage of medical cannabis, but in hindsight we know this to be untrue.

To add to all the corruption, the majority of Doctors at the time looked at all forms of cannabis as a medicine that was far better than its competitors. The critiques of the war against marijuana by medical doctors are well documented and escalated until the American Medical Association and Anslinger came to a truce. In an attempt to silence the doctors who were promoting the use of marijuana as a medicine Anslinger began to prosecute doctors for illegal distribution of narcotic drugs. After the truce the pro marihuana doctors quieted and only three doctors were prosecuted during the next decade.

Anslinger would be the head of the Federal Bureau of Narcotics from 1932 to 1962 and with the help of powerful men he was able to single handily put an end to the cultivation of hemp. For those readers who still believe politicians would never do something if it weren't in the public's best interest, I would like to bring up that Mellon also supported protective tariffs for his aluminum monopoly. The largest tariff passed up until that time was the Fordney – McCumber Tariff of 1922. In 1924 the Federal Trade Commission reported that The Aluminum Company that

Mellon still had interest in had "practically complete monopoly" and he was being shielded from foreign competition by advocating high tariffs.[59] Similar to how Henry Clay advocated protective tariffs for his hemp industry, Mellon did the same for his aluminum monopoly. The end result was higher cost for consumer products and protection from outside competition for Mellon. The Fordney – McCumber Tariff ended up creating government-assisted monopolies and led European countries to pass their own protective tariffs to retaliate against U.S. exporters. This slowed trade and was a net loss to the global economy.

Many of the men who have taken part in passing mercantilist policies have correctly been labeled *political entrepreneurs.* Instead of relying on higher quality or lower cost products these men decided to use their political power to lobby government into passing favorable legislation for their industries. Sadly, the majority of the men who have taken part in this behavior started as market entrepreneurs and transitioned to political entrepreneurs when given the opportunity to make easy money.

Hemp Politics Revisited

"Bipartisanship usually means that a larger than usual deception is being carried out." – George Carlin

The political atmosphere that Hoover and Franklin Delano Roosevelt had created leading up to the Marihuana Tax Act of 1937 was an absolute disaster. During this era of the Great Depression the popular thing to do in politics was blame business for the depression and paint government as the answer to all problems. FDR did a superb job of convincing the general public of this economic fallacy by using his fireside chats (radio broadcasts). I'm not going to dive into the reasons for the Great Depression or how little FDR actually new about economics, but I will say the depression involved the same expansion of the money supply and easy credit that has been reported during every other economic recession. The banking and business cartel that I have already discussed had a major hand in the credit expansion. Instead of ridding the world of these cartels FDR took the advice of John Maynard Keynes and blamed under consumption and lack of aggregate demand as the root causes of the depression. This was a misdiagnosis of the actual problem and it is no wonder why the Great Depression was two times longer than any other recession. FDR's answers were to expand upon many of Hoover's failed ideas and establish even stronger business cartels that were protected by the government. He also gave the banking cartel freedom to expand credit and inflate the currency in hope of creating more "aggregate demand." This didn't create more demand, but he did succeed at devaluing the dollar and decreasing the purchasing power of Americans by forty percent.[60]

FDR and Hoover believed that the economy would function better without the free market and FDR went forward passing laws to centralize power and prevent competition. His National Industrial Recovery Act revoked all previous anti-trust laws and forced businesses to work together to set prices, wages, and *even what raw materials went into making their products*. This law successfully gave power to the businesses that controlled the most market share and allowed them to write their own "fair competition" codes. These codes would then bind the entire industry to their requirements whether a producer agreed to the code or not. This allowed big businesses to set high prices and forced smaller competitors to accept these new standards even if they depended on offering a lower price to attract market share. Many small producers that depended on selling high quality low cost goods were pushed out of the market place by large national brands that had created the "fair competition" codes. Some of these smaller producers were either fined or thrown in jail if they chose to offer lower prices or broke some part of the cartel agreement. A dry cleaner from Cleveland was jailed for simply cleaning suits for five cents less than the industries agreement. Big business had in essence taken over the free market and had convinced government to enforce policies that empowered only the elite. Intellectuals that promoted these economic fallacies were thus given promotions in both academia and in the media.

Henry Ford was one business leader that believed FDR's policies were unconstitutional and he took a stand. He argued that if these policies were in place when he started his company it would have been illegal to cut cost by using the assembly line and cars would still be unaffordable to the average American citizen. He thought they allowed current businesses to maintain power and punished innovative thinkers. He wrote in his notebook, "I do not think that this country is ready to be treated like Russia for a while... There is a lot of the pioneer spirit here yet." Others in the auto industry tried to push him into signing the "fair competition" agreement to raise prices, but he would not budge. One of these men was Pierre S. DuPont of General Motors and Andrew Mellon of all people helped finance his company. FDR was so ticked by Ford not agreeing to his new policy that he announced that Ford would no longer have an agreement with the government for automobiles and that the government would pay a higher price for their fleet.[61]

To go along with the cartelization and the elimination of anti-trust laws, FDR also passed legislation to control the agriculture industry. This policy was called the Agricultural Adjustment Act and suffered the same failures as the National Industrial Recovery Act. In 1933 the U.S. began plowing under crops and killed roughly 6 million piglets in hopes that a smaller supply would raise the market price. This was going on at a time when people were looking for agriculture jobs and starving for food.[62] Luckily both these acts were ruled unconstitutional in 1935-36, but FDR continued to pass similar legislation throughout his terms. FDR was so in love with the idea of leading the National Industrial Recovery Act that he hoped to someday run an international business cartel. According to FDR's close friend and Secretary of the Treasury Henry Morgenthau, FDR

> pictures himself as being called in as a consultant of the various nations of the world. He said, "Maybe I can prescribe for their ailments or, after making a study of their illnesses, I will simply turn up my nose at them and say, 'I am sorry – I cannot treat the.' For example I would tell England that she had too many people and she should move out ten million of her population. I would take a look at each country and, of course, when we made them disarm we would have to find new work for the munitions workers in each country and that is where this international cartel would come in and your job would be to handle the finances."[63]

One can write an entire book regarding the failure of Hoover/FDR's policies and their success in establishing a more consolidated economy, but I am just trying to show that the business cartel, banking cartel, and government corruption were at a new high during the years leading up to the Marihuana Tax Act. These elite businessmen and politicians had no limits and would stop at nothing to maintain their power.

In summary, the idea of hemp being revitalized as a crop did not sit well with the executives from the chemical, wood pulp, steel, cotton, pharmaceutical, and oil cartels. These lobbyists successfully disguised the argument against industrial hemp as the war against marihuana and the rest is history.

Mercantilist policies that benefit one group over another can only make sense by employing arguments that are based on economic fallacy. By legalizing industrial hemp and influencing foreign nations to follow our example, we can begin to build a more sustainable and decentralized global economy. There is too much *untapped capital (people, ideas, raw materials)* within the industrial hemp industry to not utilize this amazing plant once again. Hemp's only threat comes from the mercantilist policies that come out of Washington.

Chemurgy Movement

Most people have never heard of the chemurgy movement that attracted some of the brightest minds in the science world during the early 20th century. Chemist William J. Hale created the term 'chemurgy' in his 1934 book *The Farm Chemurgic*. The idea that powered the chemurgy movement was the drive to develop more uses for excess farm materials in order to decentralize production and provide farmers with more profits. In 1935 the Farm Chemurgic Council was founded in an effort to develop more uses for these renewable farm materials. This new movement was perceived as a huge threat to both the business cartel and the politicians in charge. The FDR administration even viewed this new movement as a political threat.

This farming issue was so political due the government's involvement in economics and agriculture during this time. Leading up to the mid 1930s farmers had been suffering through low agriculture prices dating back to WWI. Farmers were encouraged to ramp up production during wartime and by the time WWI ended farmers were left with a glutted market and low prices. These low prices were brought on by the increase in farming efficiencies and were a disaster for rural America. Agriculture prices were hurt even more after the passage of the Smoot-Hawley Tariff that raised tariffs on over 20,000 goods to all time highs. This created retaliation tariffs in foreign countries and the result was a boycott of all American made agriculture goods.

FDR's "Brain Trust" concluded that these economic problems were the result of overproduction or under consumption. This called for government intervention to stimulate demand and/or government intervention to lower supply and thus increase prices. FDR decided to do both in order to fix the supposed problem, but his policies had little success in pulling the country out of the depression.

Instead of looking at overproduction and increases in efficiency as bad things, the chemurgy movement led by the likes of Henry Ford and George Washington Carver believed that demand for these materials should increase and replace products being made from petrochemicals. This was the exact opposite of what FDR was doing with the Agricultural Adjustment Act. The chemurgy movement stood against FDR and the AAA for distorting market prices and destroying production. Chemurgists understood that production created American prosperity and production was going to be the only thing that would improve the economic situation. Chemurgists were simply applying the economic principles of Say's Law to their problem, while many proponents of the AAA ignored this economic idea. FDR's policies of plowing up fields, slaughtering animals, and subsidizing farmers did not sit well with this group and actually resulted in a loss of wealth for Americans.

In the 1930s those that wanted to create more sustainable supply chains were cast aside as enemies to the status quo and the business cartels. The chemurgy movement believed government involvement in agriculture was only helping farmers barely survive and was just making them dependent on government handouts. Chemurgist wanted to empower farmers and allow them to create more wealth and freedom by expanding the market for their raw materials. The chemurgy movement was thus deemed a populous Republican movement and alternative to FDR's AAA. Henry Ford was quoted saying "If we industrialists want the American farmer to be our customer, we must find a way to become his customer. This is what I am working for."[64] If we hope to build an economy that is environmentally sustainable and shares the wealth, Ford's vision would be a great foundation.

Eventually in 1938 FDR passed another AAA bill and recognized the chemurgy movement and the need for laboratories to develop more agriculture demand. This new bill allocated four million dollars to be allocated equally to four new laboratories that would develop new markets for farm materials.

FDR and the American allies would later be thankful to the chemurgy movement as without this scientific push the allies would not of had enough materials to fight WWII. During war time agriculture was once again used to create anything from rubber to aviation fuel. Without the increase in farm production it is believed that D-day would not of been possible.

When the war ended the focus once again shifted away from sustainable production of materials via agriculture and toward centralized production controlled by oil cartels. The same farmers that were responsible for growing the materials to win the war were once again left behind in the post war economy. Industrial hemp not only played a big part in the chemurgy movement, but it also was a valuable material for WWII.

Hemp For Victory

After the Japanese invaded the Philippine Islands in 1942 the United States was cut off completely from the Manila hemp that was supplying a large part of the nation with fiber. The U.S. government knew right away that in order to adequately supply their troops and allies with supplies they must find a substitute for the Manila hemp. The government's solution was to distribute 400,000 pounds of hemp seeds to American farmers with an emphasis on Kentucky & Wisconsin. The U.S. government even made a fifteen-minute long documentary called Hemp For Victory that can be seen on Youtube. This reversal in domestic policy has many people scratching their head. If hemp is good during wartime, why can't it be used during times of peace? Overall it is estimated that Americans grew over 150,000 acres of hemp for the war effort.[65] The hemp material was used in an assortment of military goods including rope, webbing, and garments.

Prohibition Till Present

In 1961 the U.N. Single Convention on Narcotic Drugs said cannabis should be punished similar to opium, but made an exception for industrial hemp. The U.N. stated, "This convention shall not apply to the cultivation of cannabis plant exclusively for industrial purposes or horticultural purposes."[66] Nine years later the Controlled Substances Act of 1970 was passed in the U.S., but there was no mentioning of industrial hemp being regulated separately. The Drug Enforcement Administration was thus given the power to regulate industrial hemp. This law did not make it illegal to grow industrial hemp, but any farmer wishing to partake in the hemp industry would have to get a permit from the DEA. These permits have been nearly impossible to secure.

Between 1970 and 1993 no permits were granted, but in 1994 the Hempstead Company in California was granted a permit to grow a half an acre of hemp for fiber and seed. Midway through the growing season however the permit was ruled invalid by California Attorney General Dan Lungren and state officials were ordered to plow the field up. This same year President Clinton signed executive order 12919 that listed industrial hemp as an agricultural crop that was crucial for national security purposes.

Two years after the California sabotage the Hawaii

Industrial Hemp Research Project was granted a permit to study hemp. The research program lasted for four years and was terminated after governmental delays involving the DEA's inspection of imported seeds.[67] Part of their research found that industrial hemp could be used to clean up polycyclic aromatic hydrocarbons (pollutants linked to cancer) from contaminated soil.

The DEA has taken a ridiculous stance on industrial hemp and has attempted to increase their regulatory powers over the plant rather than liberalize it. They have even gone so far as to destroy industrial hemp being grown on Native American tribal lands (Oglala Sioux) and confiscated imported hemp products that contain non-psychoactive amounts of THC. It has been reported that 98% of cannabis sativa plants that the DEA eradicates is considered ditch weed and has no drug uses.[68] The majority of these plants that are eradicated are the offspring from the hemp fields during the Hemp for Victory campaign (WWII) and should be studied for their resilience. The fact of the matter is that these law enforcement agencies realize that they will see their federal budgets get slashed if they don't have the responsibility of pulling weeds anymore.

The DEA claims that their stance against industrial hemp is justified and says, "problems of detection and enforcement easily justify a ban broader than the psychoactive variety of the plant."[69] Historically speaking this stance just doesn't hold up. In the 1937 Marihuana Tax Act they clearly made an exception for the cultivation of industrial hemp and this was before we had the technology to test the THC content. The claim by the DEA that they would have problems of "detection and enforcement" is very hard to believe. Canada has been growing industrial hemp for the last 18 years and has not had any problems with law enforcement not being able to identify the two varieties of cannabis sativa.

Outside of the DEA most organizations are for the legalization of industrial hemp. The World Trade Organization, North American Free Trade Agreement, and the General Agreement on Tariffs and Trade all of which the U.S is involved with recognize industrial hemp. In addition, the National conference of state legislators and the National Association of State Departments of Agriculture have advised the DEA to amend their current policies on industrial hemp.[70]

Even if a farmer were granted a permit to grow industrial hemp under the DEA, it would not be profitable. The DEA would require prison style fencing surrounding the entire field, 24-7 armed security, and alarm systems. In Canada farmers are just required to use certified seed, pay for routine crop testing, report GPS coordinates of crop, pass a background check, and have enough farmland.

During the revival of the Canadian hemp industry that started in 1998, an American company called Consolidated Growers and Processors Inc. was the major contractor during the first two years. It was responsible for around 40 percent of the Canadian hemp market, but unfortunately it went bankrupt and defaulted on the majority of its obligations in 1999. This bankruptcy, combined with DEA's outlandish attempts to ban all hemp imports to the United States was a huge setback for the North American industrial hemp market. In 2004, after a drawn out legal battle with the DEA, the Canadian hemp farmers and American businessmen were victorious and industrial hemp imports and total cultivation in Canada started to increase once again. The following year a Congressional Research Service stated, "The United States is the only developed nation in which industrial hemp is not an established crop." [71]

Ever since the Canadian hemp industry won their battle with the DEA hemp imports into the United States have increased dramatically. In 2012 it was estimated by the Hemp Industries Association that the total retail value of hemp products was over a half a billion dollars. Due to the increasing demand for hemp products in the U.S., Canada is expected to increase their acreage of hemp cultivated by 10-15 percent in 2013 according to the Canadian Hemp Trade Alliance.

Economic Impact of Industrial Hemp in Kentucky

In 1998 my alma mater, the University of Kentucky conducted an economic feasibility report on the revival of the industrial hemp industry in Kentucky. Dr. Eric C. Thompson, Dr. Mark C. Berger, and Steven N. Allen spearheaded the investigation. Even after taking conservative estimates they still found industrial hemp could bring in more revenue to farmers than the 14 most common crops grown in Kentucky except tobacco. I was going to leave this section out of my book, but after hearing in early 2013 that opponents of hemp wanted to see more economic studies I had to toss in this short synopsis. The following is a summary of their findings.

The report found that Kentucky could become one of the states to benefit the most from introducing industrial hemp. It is believed that Kentucky will hold a comparative advantage over other states due to its history, long growing seasons, appropriate soil conditions, and its large horse racing industry. The prominent horse racing industry would become buyers of industrial hemp for bedding and seed meal for horse feed. Establishing processing centers and farmland in this area would benefit the farmers and producers by eliminating a large portion of transportation expenses occurred while getting hemp products to market.

The hemp industry would also benefit many rural communities where unemployment has devastated once thriving communities. Due to the bulkiness of hemp fiber it is not economically feasible to transport large amounts of hemp over 50 miles. As a result, the hemp industry would have to remain decentralized and could not depend on shipping raw materials across state lines or up to Canada to be processed. The new industry would help lower and stabilize unemployment figures and create many more jobs around the community after applying the multiplier effect. According to the report "If just one-fourth of Kentucky's 90 agricultural counties went into industrial hemp business, approximately 17,348 jobs would be created and $396 million in worker earning generated yearly."

This study looked at the different markets for hemp, potential markets for hemp in the future, cost incurred for cultivating hemp, return for growing hemp, detailed analysis of the processing and manufacturing need, and the amount of potential jobs needed to maintain a thriving hemp industry.

It was estimated in 1998 that farmers could earn a profit of $320 per acre for hemp straw (the trunk of the plant) production, $220 for growing hemp seed, and $600 for growing certified hemp seed used for planting the following years crop. It is important to note that these returns would most likely diminish as more and more hemp farmers entered the market place. As supply increases farmers will most likely lower their bids to guarantee contracts with the local processing centers (Farmers should only grow industrial hemp if they have a contract with a producer). As prices lower per ton it is also likely that there will be higher yields per acre as farmers learn which seeds work best. The increase in yield will help prices from falling to drastically per acre. The fall in prices per ton and increase in tons per acre will allow more businesses to look at supplementing their current raw materials with hemp. This increase in demand will thus push more farmland into hemp production.

The report also studied four possible scenarios that could happen in Kentucky. First, Kentucky could become the main supplier for certified hemp seed (growing certified seed does not require the expensive processing plants that growing hemp straw does). In this scenario it would give Kentucky an estimated 69 full-time jobs and $1,300,000 in worker earnings. Second, if one hemp-processing center (processes hemp fiber) is located in Kentucky and farmers were allowed to cultivate certified seed this would give Kentucky 303 fulltime jobs with $6,700,000 in worker earnings. Third, if two processing centers were located in Kentucky 537 fulltime jobs would be created and $12,100,000 in worker earnings. Fourth, if one processing plant and one hemp paper pulp factory were built there would be 771 fulltime jobs created and $17,600,000 in worker earnings.

Chapter 3: The Most Versatile Plant in the World

"I believe that the great Creator has put ores and oil on this earth to give us a breathing spell. As we exhaust them, we must be prepared to fall back on our farms, which is God's true storehouse and can never be exhausted. We can learn to synthesize material for every human need from things that grow." – George Washington Carver

"We must be the change we wish to see in the world." – Mahatma Gandhi

Many hemp enthusiasts like to claim that hemp is a miracle crop that was created to save all of humanity. This makes for a good story and high expectations, but is far from the truth. The real story is that estimating what America's hemp industry could accomplish is hard to do simply because there are few proven facts and little research is being done. *The hemp industry will be whatever hemp entrepreneurs and conscious consumers make it.*

Using conservative estimates we can say with confidence that American farmers could expect to see 3-5 tons of hemp stems per acre, but what really matters is the quality of the plant. There are four different materials that are produced from industrial hemp. Long Fiber: Similar to cotton in its uses, but is stronger and has anti-mildew and antimicrobial characteristics. This fiber is great for all sorts of textiles. Medium Fiber: Has the same anti-mildew and antimicrobial characteristics as long fiber, but is not suited for all textiles due to its shorter length. This fiber is perfect for making paper products since it has a low amount of lignin (binder). Short core fiber: One of the most absorbent materials in the world and is often used in animal bedding and environmentally friendly construction materials. Seed: One of the healthiest nuts you can eat and easy on the digestive tract. This seed can also be crushed for its oil and the residue can be used for protein, flour, or animal feeds.

The long fiber makes up around 25 to 35 percent of the plant, but the percentage of usable long fiber depends mostly on the technology being implemented to separate the fibers. The four main characteristics that end up determining the value of each hemp crop are seed yield, fiber length, cellulose, and the amount of lignin (stuff that holds the plant together).[72]

After the long fiber is separated, the remaining part of the plant is made up of shorter fibers that are perfect for replacing wood products. The long-term success of the

American hemp industry will largely depend on how we develop markets for the shorter fibers as opposed to the longer fibers.

Once industrial hemp becomes legal to farm in the United States farmers will see a gradual increase in total yields as more research and selective plant breeding is implemented. Some farmers could even see their tonnage per acre double after just a few years of plant development. Plant breeders will not only be looking for an increase in yield, but they will also be looking for certain characteristics. Breeders will attempt to create plants that have a higher percentage of long fiber, yield more seeds, or have a higher essential fatty acid profile. These improvements could have a huge impact on the profitability of certain hemp industries and bring more money to hemp farmers.

As it stands now, government interventions in the market place have cost farmers a valuable crop and have denied manufactures a raw material that could replace unsustainable materials. John W. Roulac says it best in his book *Hemp Horizons: The Comeback of the World's Most Promising Plant,* "The official exclusion of industrial hemp from the federal government-approved list of fiber resources impedes buyers and sellers from using the raw goods of their choice. This is tantamount to a **socialist or communist** policy whereby the state, at its sole discretion, determines which fiber resources can compete and which are prohibited."[73]

The prohibition of hemp is a perfect example of how government regulations have hurt the consumer as well as the environment. When governments get into the business of picking winners and losers the public at large always ends up with less choices, less liberties, and in this case a downgrade in environmental standards. The winners are always the well-connected political entrepreneurs that need protection from substitute goods.

If hemp were legalized in the United States it is estimated that farmers could produce the raw materials for over 25,000 products. All of these products can be made in America and be manufactured more responsibly than their alternatives. As worldwide fiber prices continue to go up due to increases in population and increase in demand, industrial hemp will be looked at more and more as a viable option. Consumers are not only looking for durable products, but sustainable manufacturing will play a key part in where consumer's money goes.

Could hemp play a part in the replacement of timber and cotton? Realistically hemp probably won't be the only fiber to replace these materials, but it can definitely grab a large market share. The demand for hemp will continue to increase as more "green labels" hit the marketplace.

Marketing and advertising companies are on the leading edge of the sustainability movement and they have quickly realized that the characteristics associated with industrial hemp make marketing to knowledgeable consumers a breeze. More people are realizing the differences between industrial hemp and marijuana and believe that there is nothing controversial about using hemp products. In my opinion the use of imported petrochemical products is much more controversial than the use of sustainable raw materials.

As we progress as a nation, the top business talent will begin to move toward sustainable industries. It is much easier and much more rewarding marketing a product that could slow the destruction of ancient forests, provide eco-friendly clothing, slow the importation of foreign petrochemicals, support small farms and rural communities and creates less pollution than its competitors. Money aside who would want to go to a company to market a product or service that pollutes the environment, makes you fat and unhealthy, or serves no purpose other than make a quick buck? Entrepreneurs such as Yvon Chouinard of Patagonia are leading the way in this new style of business. People like Yvon and other sustainable entrepreneurs are realizing that they can make money while also making the world a better place.

Savvy and knowledgeable consumers range across all generations and they are demanding sustainability and durability. Over the past decade people can easily see changes in the way businesses are going about their daily activities. The market is quickly approaching the sustainability tipping point. This point will usher in the era of sustainable business practices and will create wealth and prosperity to those who seek to be a part of it. This point could be 6 months down the road, 2 years, or it might even take a full decade, but there is no stopping what the consumer wants. The biggest factor in bringing about a more sustainable economy will be how well these new companies spread their messages via their social media networks. The beauty about the marketplace is that a once thriving billion-dollar corporation can lose market share and go bankrupt within a few short months if they don't listen to what the consumer wants. Businesses must always be innovating to meet the consumer's needs and social media has given consumers and citizens a bigger platform to voice their needs.

As we approach this sustainability tipping point people need to realize that this is not a gradual increase in sustainability or a linear increase, but is an exponential increase in sustainability and we are just getting started. We are on the verge of one of the biggest changes in the way businesses operate since the industrial revolution. Businesses, nor the government will lead this change, but American consumers will lead the way by voting with their dollars and forcing businesses to adopt the appropriate values.

The exponential growth in sustainable thinking will be driven by generation Y or millennials who are more environmentally conscious than previous generations and are known for their early acceptance of new products. As this generation's income begins to rise businesses will begin to see more and more shoppers voting with their dollars. This push toward natural, organic, and sustainable products will force businesses and farmers to change the way they operate. Businesses that speculate and meet this need first will be rewarded with happy customers.

Since we have a pretty good idea of what consumers want and what they are going to be demanding in the future, it's my job as an entrepreneur to figure out how to fulfill those needs. The reason I decided to take up the challenge of starting a company encompassing a product that is currently not allowed to be cultivated was its problem solving potential. I saw a raw material that could play a major part in our quest to becoming a more sustainable and healthier world.

America has led the free world in innovation during the last 200 years and I see no change in the entrepreneurial attitude that makes America great. We are also the world's largest economy and wield the power to change the way businesses conduct themselves, what products they produce, and what raw materials and inputs are used.

Industrial hemp is not the sole answer to our economy or our sustainability problems, but I believe it can be an important piece of the pie. With over 25,000 potential uses it will not be short of potential markets. The top industries that could capitalize on the reintroduction of industrial hemp are the automobile, construction, cosmetics, food, plastic, and textile industries. For the rest of this chapter I will be discussing the versatility of this amazing plant and what industries could potentially develop with more research and development.

Textiles

"When a great truth once gets abroad in the world, no power on earth can imprison it, or prescribe its limits, or suppress it. It is bound to go on till it becomes the thought of the world. Such a truth is women's right to equal liberty with man" – Fredrick Douglas

Historically the textile industry had been dominated by hemp, but with the rise of mechanical innovations during the late 19th and 20th century hemp took a back seat to cotton and polyester substitutes. Both of these substitutes have shown to be some of the most pollutant, energy intensive, and water intensive products on the market. Just during the manufacturing process polyester needs on average six times the energy when compared to hemp or cotton production.[74] Cotton isn't much better and uses more agrochemicals and water than any other crop in the world. According to research done by The World Wildlife Fund in 2005, 2.4 percent of the Earth's farmland is planted with cotton, but it requires nearly a quarter of the total insecticides used each year and 11 percent of total pesticides.[75] These numbers have been similar in recent years. Cotton's second most used insecticide called Aldicarb can even kill a human by attacking and paralyzing the respiratory system. Even more shocking is that Aldicarb has been found in the groundwater of 16 states.[76]

In his book *The Responsible Company,* Yvon Chouinard (founder of Patagonia) stresses the unsustainable practice of using nonorganic cotton in clothing. When discussing the cotton growing process he writes, "It's a horrific story. To prepare soil for planting cotton, workers spray organophosphates (which can damage the human central nervous system) to kill off all other living organisms. The soil, once treated, is doornail dead (five pesticide-free years have to pass before earthworms, an indication of soil health, can return). Such soil requires intensive use of artificial fertilizers to hold the cotton plants in place. Rainwater runoff from cotton fields contributes significantly to the growth of ocean dead zones."[77] This is some pretty scary information considering United States is the second largest producer of cotton in the world, accounting for just under 20% of the world's total crop.[78] Demand for cotton fibers is also expected to double by 2030.

The use of chemicals on cotton crops not only effects our environment, but our own health as well. In a controversial study done in 2005, David Pimentel claimed that spraying pesticides in America cost $1.1 billion per year in health costs, $1.5 billion per year due to "super pests" created from multiple years of spraying and $1.4 billion in crop losses due to pesticides. The controversial part of his report is when he assigned monetary values to items that did not have established prices such as a $2.2 billion loss due to bird deaths and a $2 billion dollar loss due to pesticides contaminating groundwater.[79]

Agrochemical spaying isn't the only controversial aspect about growing cotton. The introduction of biotechnology (BT) cotton was intended to lower the amount of insecticides by putting the insecticide into the plants DNA. The result has been a new wave of "superpests" that have become immune to the insecticides that are released from within the plant.[80] The rise of the "superpests" has led to an increase in spraying with no benefit it total yield.

In regards to agriculture production, hemp requires very little or even no chemicals applied to it and the crop can actually be a net benefit to the environment as opposed to a disaster. Each year it is estimated that cotton fields alone contribute 165 million metric tons of dangerous gases to the atmosphere.[81] This does not include the emissions during the transportation and processing of the cotton fibers. It has been estimated that to produce the typical cotton t-shirt just under one pound of cotton is needed and over 5 oz of man-made fertilizers could be sprayed just to produce that one pound of cotton.[82]

Overall the textile industry is one of biggest polluters and energy users in the world. The World Bank estimated that around 20 percent of corporate water pollution comes from the dyeing and processing of textiles.[83] Many industry experts believe that a transition to non-cotton fibers, such as hemp, could go a long way in helping create a more sustainable textile industry.

The developing world seeks to benefit the most from a shift to alternative fibers. 99% of the world's cotton farmers reside in developing countries and consequently have to live with the health and environmental damages of growing cotton.[84] Many proponents of cotton cite the economic benefits that cotton brings to these impoverished nations, but these areas could easily transition to hemp fiber production if given the opportunity. Industrial hemp could potentially be a strong catalyst in creating more sustainable supply chains in these countries while also improving their overall health. According to Jaideep Hardikar with the *Daily News and Analysis,* in 2009 17,638 cotton farmers in India committed suicide due to indebtedness. Hemp could help alleviate this problem since in requires a small amount of inputs and would keep farmers from having to take out unaffordable loans.

Due to the increase in consumer awareness to environmental issues, many apparel companies have begun the process of switching to organic cotton. This may seem like a better option when compared only to conventional cotton, but organic cotton is far from being sustainable. Cotton's biggest environmental strain comes from its immense water usage. When compared to industrial hemp the cotton plant uses roughly 50% more water and reports have shown that organic cotton can even demand higher amounts of water. According to the nonprofit Water Foot Print, a cotton t-shirt uses on average 660 gallons of water. Some industry experts claim hemp t-shirts could save 300 gallons of water per t-shirt, while other studies have shown that when processing is factored in hemp uses 75% less water than cotton.[85] The water foot print of cotton differs depending on where you are growing it, but nearly 75% of cotton crops are grown on irrigated land where groundwater pumping is subsidized by governments. This groundwater pumping has led to a decrease in water table levels and even caused the desertification of areas in developing countries. Subsidizing the pumping of groundwater and re-allocating fresh water flows to grow cotton in places that don't receive adequate amounts of rain are bad policies that should be stopped immediately. Fresh water that is taken from groundwater or surface water such as lakes and rivers leads to eutrophication, pollution, salinisation and destruction of habitat. Irrigation is also extremely inefficient with over half the water being lost due to seepage and evaporation.

The most well known case study of cotton irrigation completely destroying an ecosystem and its people occurred over the last 60 years in Muynak, Uzbekistan on the Aral Sea. Central planners in the former Soviet Union began diverting water from the Ama Dariya and the Syrdariya rivers to irrigate their cotton fields. The diversion of water caused the 4th largest inland sea to be turned almost completely into a desert. Since the draining of the Aral Sea and the collapse of their fishing economy farmers have made modest changes, but the citizens still depend on the struggling cotton industry. Any recovery in water levels is going at a snails pace. To go along with the collapse of their ecosystem heavy usage of agrochemicals along with excess salt have contaminated the drinking water. Cancer and disease rates are higher throughout the area. The deputy mayor Togian Ibragimova warns, "It could easily happen again and again. Human beings can be very stupid."[86]

To go along with cotton's high water use, cotton also demands more farmland to yield the same amount of fiber.

On average hemp yields around 250% more fiber per acre. Cotton's high demand for farmland can only be met in areas with sub-tropical climates and where large portions of our food crops compete for acreage. Hemp can be grown in all 50 states and this fact alone could help pave the way for decentralized rural textile manufacturers. This could dramatically reduce the transportation and energy used from shipping textiles halfway across the world. The difference between cotton and hemp yields is even more extreme when comparing organic hemp and cotton. Growing organic hemp on a commercial scale is much easier than growing organic cotton due to hemp's pest resistance. If all clothing designers unanimously decided they would only use organic cotton, farmers would have to increase cotton acreage 20-50%. This would lead to more groundwater depletion and the deforestation of areas in sub-tropical climates to make more farmland. With demand for cotton predicted to double by 2030, the idea of organically growing cotton needs to be reassessed. Many people might look at synthetic fibers to pick up some of the added demand, but with high-energy prices in the future and oil being non-renewable this option also looks bleak. Alternative fibers such as hemp and flax look to be in the best position to meet added fiber demand.

In the past hemp textiles were often coarse and very similar to linen materials, but in recent years new technologies have been invented that turn hemp into softer fibers that are similar to cotton. Currently, the processing of alternative fibers is a bottleneck in the hemp textile industry, but companies like Crailar are quickly implementing the technology that turns long bast fibers in flax, kenaf, jute and hemp into quality textile fibers. Crailar is currently focusing on flax, but their technology could easily be turned toward processing industrial hemp fibers upon legalization. When comparing water usage, flax performs better than cotton, but is not as efficient as hemp.[87]

To go along with hemp's environmental benefits hemp clothing is also three times more durable than cotton, is UV resistant, has better antibacterial properties than cotton, can be blended with other natural fibers, and can eventually become cost effective once allowed to be grown in the United States.

Bioplastics & Hemp

"By replacing materials that were hard to find or expensive to process, celluloid (first thermoplastic) democratized a host of goods for an expanding consumption oriented middle class." – Historian Jeffrey Meikle[88]

Plastics are arguably one of mankind's most important inventions. They can be found in virtually every consumer product and have replaced many expensive metals in the supply chain. Consequently, plastics make up a large portion of total landfill use and it is estimated that around 5% of the world's production of plastic ends up in the ocean.[89]

In the coming decades the bioplastic industry is going to play an important role in creating more sustainable supply chains. Bioplastics are simply made from polymers resulting from the cultivation or collection of biomass as opposed to petrochemicals. Some of the leading bioplastic crops are soy, corn, sugar cane, potato starch, tree cellulose, and farm waste. If industrial hemp were legalized, manufacturers would instantly be interested in using hemp as one of their top options.

One of the biggest misconceptions about the bioplastics industry is that all bioplastics are biodegradable. Many bioplastics can be composted naturally while other bioplastics need to go to an industrial composting plant. A large portion of the bioplastics used in consumer products (not packaging) and industrial uses can even compare to conventional plastic when it comes to durability and versatility. These plastics are often the bioplastics that are not biodegradable. Bioplastics that do not biodegrade are often looked at as a plus however since they permanently remove carbon from the air. The biodegradable bioplastics are often used in packaging to help eliminate waste and environmental degradation.

In 2011 in was estimated that the world's annual output of plastic was 225 million tons. Of this 225 million tons bioplastics made up roughly 0.5%. It is also estimated that 4% of the world's oil is consumed by the plastic industry to make the very products that can be grown from our farm fields. Even though bioplastics make up a very small percentage of current plastic, the bioplastic industry has a bright future and has been growing by at least 20% per year over the last few years. The economic advantage that the petrochemical industry has is rapidly diminishing as high oil prices drive up the cost of conventional plastics and economics of scale are realized in the bioplastic industry. The majority of bioplastics are currently two times more expensive than conventional plastics, but some plastics produced in Brazil out of sugar cane have nearly matched the conventional plastic industry in price.[90] Many businessmen are also finding it beneficial from a public relations standpoint to pay the premium on bioplastic in order to have a more sustainable image. This is the market working and evolving to meet consumer's needs.

Nestle is one of the many organizations that are currently taking a hard look at bioplastics for their packaging options. The head of their packaging design, Dr. Anne Roulin says, "I think it is going to be an evolution where we will continuously reduce environmental impact and find more energy efficient processes. But I really see the trend going in the direction of conventional plastics made from renewable resources."[91] Entire cities are also joining the bioplastics revolution. Good luck finding a conventional plastic utensil in Seattle, city ordinances are making restaurants provide only biodegradable forks, spoons, knifes, and sporks.

One company that is investing in bioplastics is DOW chemical company in Brazil. They are looking to create competitively priced bioplastics using renewable sugar cane. The DOW facility can hold 240 million liters of ethanol that will eventually be converted into thousands of tons of polyethylene, the most common plastic in the world. [92] Hemp could easily be transformed into a bioplastic crop that produces comparable amounts of ethanol for bioplastics. The process of creating plastics from ethanol is not a new concept and has actually been around since the 1920s. It is important to note that DOW has tried investing in corn bioplastics, but pulled out in 2005 due to failure to make ends meet. Hemp needs to be legalized so private industries can help develop the American bioplastics market with the most efficient plants. Our planet and our sustainability issues are too important to handcuff entrepreneurs from using the most versatile plant in the world.

Just like energy crops, crops being grown for bioplastics will often be questioned on land use, increasing food prices, water usage, and the potential for deforestation. The fact of the matter is using biomass to produce plastics would be much easier than using biomass for energy. According to energy and environmental author Chris Goodall, the "world's plastic industry is only about one tenth the size of the transport fuels sector in terms of its use of oil. If today's entire plastics production derived from biological sources it would consume between 0.1% and 0.2% of the globe's total annual production of organic matter... Even if half the world's plastics were made from crops grown on food land, the industry would only require 3% of the world's cultivated acreage."[93] Bioplastics can also be created from thinning forests for cellulose and harvesting algae, which doesn't require land.

One of the cutting edge bioplastic producers in Brazil has created even more efficiency by powering their manufacturing plant with the biomass that is not used for plastic production. This eliminates the use of nonrenewable energy sources and creates a product that can actually sequester more carbon from the air.

In 2011 the market for bioplastics in North America was roughly 300,00 metric tons and it is expected to quadruple by 2016. In hopes to meet this estimate, On April 26, 2012 the Obama Administration announced that they would be committing to "strengthening bioscience research as a major driver of American innovation and economic growth."[94] This is important as it shows that the government is somewhat competent when it comes to understanding the importance of our bioeconomy, but it is somewhat disappointing that the majority of the research funds will be going to government affiliated research facilities that focus on crops that are water intensive, agrochemical intensive, and subsidized by tax payers.

The report goes on to say, "A growing U.S. population requires increased health services and more material resources including food, animal feed, fiber for clothing and housing, and sources of energy and chemicals for manufacturing. Recent advances in the biological sciences are allowing more and more of these needs to be met not with petroleum-based products and other non-renewable resources but with materials that are quite literally home-grown." To me it sounds like the government should be jumping at the opportunity to legalize industrial hemp since it can fulfill all of the requirements listed for a growing U.S. population.

Bioplastics can be manufactured using plant starch, lignin, cellulose, oils, and proteins. Hemp could be a factor in all of these plastic processes and would be a great asset to the bioplastics industry. The fastest growing application for hemp fiber is in blending polypropylene with hemp fiber to create a working part. One industry that is expected to reap huge benefits from the development of bioplastics and natural fibers is the automobile industry. Some experts even believe the auto industry could be the buyers for 25% of the worlds bioplastic supply by 2025.

Automobiles

Fifteen years ago the use of industrial hemp was unheard of in the auto world, but currently BMW, Ford, GM, Honda, Mitsubishi, Porsche, Mercedes (C-class averages around 30 hemp parts per vehicle) and Volkswagen are leading the way in creating more sustainable designs using hemp. These companies utilize hemp in making interior seats, insulation, injection molds, and a few companies are even using hemp for structural panels due to its amazing strength. This increase in hemp usage can partially be credited with the added emphasis on recycling across the world. Hemp fibers are much easier to reuse and less energy is required when compared to conventional fibers.

Hemp and kenaf are the two leading natural fibers being used in the automobile industry, but researchers from Belgium have found that hemp outperforms kenaf in impact tests.[95] Hemp is also made up of 56-66% of cellulose verses 46-57% in kenaf, hemp has a lower water requirement when compared to kenaf, and 35.5% of hemp's total biomass is dry matter verses only 17.1% in kenaf.[96] The higher dry matter percentage means less money spent drying out the crop, as well as lower transportation costs. Many in the industry believe that demand for hemp would increase if there were a more reliable supply.

In an effort to reduce the amount of petrochemicals used in manufacturing, many engineers have begun using plant cellulose to create their plastic parts. Hemp along with other natural fibers could realistically be implemented as the input to create all of the necessary plastics in automobiles. The use of hemp or other plants with high cellulose also translates into a drop in energy bills as less energy is exerted during the processing of these materials. To go along with a drop in energy bills natural fibers are also easier on the processing equipment and result in less wear and tear.[97] After replacing their glass-fiber components with hemp-reinforced materials Ford reported a 31 percent reduction in total CO_2 emissions for the Mondeo sedan.[98] Natural fibers such as hemp are also around 25 percent lighter than similar synthetics while being 25 percent stronger.[99] This creates a safer more fuel-efficient vehicle. Hemp plastics also aid in CO_2 sequestration through the lifetime of the product while petrochemical plastics produce CO_2.

One of the most sustainable concept cars built in recent years is the Eco Elise, built by Lotus Engineering. The idea behind the Elise was to reduce the carbon footprint not only through the exhaust pipe, but also during the manufacturing process. One of its most important materials is industrial hemp that is grown locally near the Lotus Engineering manufacturing facilities. The seat composites and fabric, the floor mats, outer panels of the car, the spoiler, and racing stripe going down the center of the car are all made from hemp. Two solar panels have even been implanted into the hemp made hardtop to help charge the electric system. [100]

Ford Motor Company disclosed their use of hemp in their 2008/09 sustainability report:

"We are also developing fiber composites a substitute for the glass fibers traditionally used in plastic automotive components to make them stronger. For example, we are assessing the possibility of substituting up to 30 percent of the glass-fiber reinforcement in injection-molded plastics with sisal and hemp natural fibers. These parts have competitive mechanical and thermal properties and good surface appearance, and can be cost competitive. These natural-fiber reinforced parts also reduce vehicle weight significantly and reduce life-cycle CO_2 emissions, compared to glass-fiber-reinforced parts." [101]

Using industrial hemp and natural fiber is not a new idea for the Ford Motor Company, but is simply a forgotten idea that is being resurrected. In the 1930s and 40s Henry Ford experimented using plant biomass to make car panels. Ford found that these panels were lighter and more dent resistant than conventional panels. An analysis in 2002 by Purdue University reports, "Henry Ford recognized the utility of hemp in early times. In advance of today's automobile manufacturers, he constructed a car with certain components made of resin stiffened with hemp fiber."[102] It is believed that Henry Ford's original vision consisted of growing all his raw materials from local farm fields as opposed to mining and destroying nature's beauty. If Americans really wanted to revitalize our automobile industry, Ford's vision might be a good place to start.

A December 1941 Popular Mechanics article documented one of Ford's many prototypes. "When Henry Ford recently unveiled his plastic car, result of 12 years of research, he gave the world a glimpse of the automobile of tomorrow, its tough panels molded under hydraulic pressure of 1,500 pounds per square inch from a recipe that calls for 70 percent of cellulose fibers from wheat straw, hemp and sisal plus 30 percent resin binder. The only steel in the car is its tubular welded frame. The plastic car weighs a ton, 1,000 pounds lighter than a comparable steel car. Manufactures are already talking of a low-priced plastic car to test the public's taste by 1943."[103]

Even though Ford and other American companies are utilizing hemp in their vehicles, they have to deal with the unnecessary burden of higher prices due to importation of this raw material. In recent months manufacturers for Toyota have expressed interest in using industrial hemp in some of their components if hemp became legal.[104] The fact that American farmers can't grow their own hemp crops puts American automobile companies at a disadvantage in making more sustainable and fuel-efficient vehicles. If the hemp market developed in America it would give all manufacturers the incentive to use more sustainable and homegrown materials. One of the major problems in adopting industrial hemp into products is the variability and inconsistency in the market. By creating a home market for industrial hemp this will help stabilize the supply and increase the demand for industrial hemp. This is a win for farmers, manufacturers, the environment, and most of all consumers will benefit by having cheaper, safer, and better products.

Canada, a country not known for its automobile manufacturing is trying to show the world the impact industrial hemp can have on the manufacturing industry. A company out of Calgary Alberta called Motive Industries released a prototype car made from hemp and powered off of electric batteries. This car called the Kestrel was first revealed during an Electric Vehicle Conference and Trade Show in September 2010 and the designers are currently looking for a manufacturing partner to mass-produce the vehicle. The car sits four people and is a three-door hatchback. One of the main drawbacks of this vehicle is also one of its best marketing advantages. The zero emissions it creates only makes it useful for city driving and it is only expected to get 25-100 miles per charge, depending on the battery. Even with these flaws, Motive Industries is one of the great examples of how industrial hemp can provide a vision and new direction to the automobile industry. During the design stages Motive partnered with polytechnic schools to attract research funds from the Canadian government and also to educate students about the possibilities of industrial hemp. Nathan Armstrong, President of Motive Industries claims that compared to fiberglass, hemp has roughly the same performance, its 10 percent lighter, and 20 percent less expensive. Armstrong believes in future years this price advantage will continue to increase and states "the true cost of synthetic fibers isn't known, as the whole industry is subsidized and based on huge economies of scale. To make fiberglass a massive furnace is needed and to make carbon fiber all sorts of nasty chemicals and acids are used – plus big furnaces. Natural fibers = seed + water + sunlight."[105] In other words, governments all over the world simply need to stop subsidizing the industries that compete with industrial hemp and other natural fibers. When these mercantilist government policies and subsidizes are reversed we will see a surge in real sustainable economic growth. Until this happens we will continue to see environmental problems arise.

A report from Michigan State University titled, *Are natural fiber composites environmentally superior to glass fiber reinforced composites?*, concluded that natural fibers are superior to glass fibers. The abstract reads as followed:

"Natural fibers are emerging as low cost, lightweight and apparently environmentally superior alternatives to glass fibers in composites. We review select comparative life cycle assessment studies of natural fiber and glass fiber composites, and identify key drivers of their relative environmental performance. Natural fiber composites are likely to be environmentally superior to glass fiber composites in most cases for the following reasons: (1) natural fiber production has lower environmental impacts compared to glass fiber production; (2) natural fiber composites have higher fiber content for equivalent performance, reducing more polluting base polymer content; (3) the light-weight natural fiber composites improve fuel efficiency and reduce emissions in the use phase of the component, especially in auto applications; and (4) end of life incineration of natural fibers results in recovered energy and carbon credits."[106]

Many leaders in the American automobile industry already see the true potential hemp has. These men and women can't do it on their own however and they need the governments help to empower our American farmers to meet their demands. This new market is not going to be built over night, but as a country we need to start taking advantage of this renewable resource.

Hemp Biofuels

"It has been estimated that by planting only 6% of the continental U.S., we could provide for America's oil and gas requirements, thereby shifting our dependency toward renewable raw materials and energy independence. By allowing hemp to be grown in the U.S., the agriculture sector would be strengthened and farming practices could become more profitable and sustainable, creating more job opportunities in renewable sustainable hemp-related industries . . .Although the versatility of hemp increases the potential development of numerous products for human consumption and industrial applications, much research is still required" – Dr. Shelby F. Thames of The University of Southern Mississippi, Thames-Rawlins Research Group

We've learned hemp can be used to build automobiles, but it can also be used to power them. Hemp's biomass can now be turned into methanol fuel or biogas for transportation, as well as provide energy for factories and homes. Hemp can even be used to make dirty coal cleaner. Biomass such as hemp can be burned with coal stocks to reduce emissions of sulfur and carbon dioxide. This process is called cofiring and it is the most cost efficient way to utilize biomass for energy. Many experts in the field believe cofiring could be utilized on a more wide scale to help transition our economy to a more sustainable carbon neutral energy system. When compared to other energy crops, a study in northern Europe found hemp performed equal if not better than its competitors. Hemp's advantage can be found in its low energy input and high biomass output. Hemp's energy efficiencies are highest in solid biofuel, as biogas and methanol requires more energy input to produce.

One of the countries leading the way in utilizing hemp biofuel is Sweden. They have created a niche industry that processes hemp biomass into briquettes that can be burned at private households. This process also helps to decentralize the energy grid. The countries that look to benefit the most from cultivating crops like industrial hemp are the developing countries of the world. Cultivating industrial hemp would not only put people to work, but could provide a more reliable and clean energy source that could help lift countries out of poverty.

In recent years biomass has been the fastest growing supply for renewable energy. The most prominent reasons for the growth in this sector include the potential to reduce greenhouse gas emissions, the goal to become independent from foreign oil, and the possibility of lowering unemployment in rural areas. The biggest disadvantage of using biomass for energy is its low energy density when compared to fossil fuels. This low energy density means that cultivating energy crops on a large scale could put an unnecessary burden on our farmland.

Biomass for energy or fiber usage can be separated into

two classes. The first class is often called residue biomass, which is the leftover biomass from harvesting trees for pulp, farm waste and forest thinning. The second class of biomass is from crops that are specifically cultivated for energy usage. Biomass cultivated for energy consumption has a major advantage over residual biomass since it is a constant and more reliable source. On the flip side energy crops have to be cost and land efficient, where residual crops have little economic expense.

Utilizing industrial hemp to create biofuels could have a real future due to its ability to improve soil condition, no or low agrochemical usage, requires little water outside of rainwater, and is the perfect crop to use in a crop rotation. Currently many crops used for energy production have the problem of utilizing to many inputs such as water and agrochemicals. This has led many researchers to claim that biofuels don't have a future and therefore do little to eliminate the use of fossil fuels. The majority of these studies have come from research done on energy (chemically) intensive crops such as wheat and corn. One of the great qualities of industrial hemp is that it has so many by-products. Hemp can be grown for fiber to produce textiles and the leftover residual mass (close to 2/3rds of biomass) could be used to create biofuel or other consumer products.

To better understand the true potential of hemp biofuel it is important to understand the basic types of biofuels that are consumed. Biogas is a fuel produced through a process called anaerobic digestion. This is simply a sequence of steps where microorganism break down biomass in an environment depleted of oxygen. Biogas is often used in gas boilers or turbines to create heat and energy. It can also be used in the transportation industry and its byproducts can be used as fertilizers for future crops. Bio ethanol is created through a fermentation process where oxygen may or may not be present. The most well-known bio ethanol is made in Brazil out of sugar cane. Ethanol is also made out of corn in the United States, but this is extremely inefficient when compared to sugar cane. The most common use for bio ethanol is as an additive to gasoline made from fossil fuel. The fermentation process can also create other sources of energy such as methanol and acetone.

The newest improvement in developing ethanol through fermentation has been the development of utilizing lignocellulosic biomass. Previous processes to create ethanol had relied solely on sugar and grain feedstock that had to compete with food crops. Lignocellulosic biomass is believed to be the future of ethanol production and is much more abundant in residue biomass. The use of hemp hurds that are high in lignocellulose could be a perfect fit.

Hemp seed oil can also be used to create high quality bio-diesel. Researchers at the University of Connecticut believe hemp oil bio-diesel could play a huge role in creating a sustainable biofuel industry. Like other researchers they state the most important aspect for creating a feasible industry is using plants that don't displace food crops and hemp fits that mold. The use of hemp oil to create bio-diesel showed an astounding 97% conversion rate and held up better than any other bio-diesel on the market when exposed to cold temperatures. Richard Parnas a researcher at UCONN claimed that a farmer growing hemp could potentially power their entire farm off the hemp seeds collected.[107]

In reality utilizing hemp seeds to produce bio-diesel will probably not happen due to the high prices that organic food suppliers pay for the nutritious seeds. Arthur Hanks the executive director at Canadian Hemp Trade Alliance states in an article for Bio-diesel Magazine, "People talk about it, but there's not really anything happening with that right now." If hemp bio-fuel is going to have a future it will most likely come from residue biomass and lignocellulosic biomass as opposed to making bio-diesel from hemp seeds.

Hemp & Wind Power

Bio-fuel is not the only renewable energy sector that hemp is involved with. At UNC Charlotte assistant professor Na Lu and her fellow researchers are working on developing a natural composite to aid energy production for wind turbines. The team is looking to combine hemp, fiberglass, and epoxy to create lighter turbine blades. On their website Dr. Lu claims "Hemp is about 66 percent lighter than fiberglass, which provides critical weight savings for wind turbines. It also has higher storage modulus, which makes it less likely to fail."[108]

Hemp Construction Materials

An area in the construction industry that is doing well encompasses using natural fibers such as hemp to create eco-friendly building materials. In recent years this has become one of the most profitable industries for using industrial hemp in Europe. Hemp construction products do well in environments with high humidity, can be used for insulation, and are some of the strongest materials a designer can use.

Hemp's true value in construction is that it can be used as

a substitute to many products that are burdensome to the environment. Hemp products are easier to work with, safer for employees, have competitive manufacturing costs, have a longer lifecycle, can be recycled easier, and are lighter weight while maintaining strength and durability.

As people become more conscious about how their own lifestyles affect their surroundings, it will become more important to be able to deliver reliable and eco-friendly building products. Eco-friendly building products should have the following traits, be made from a renewable resource, raw material needs to be plentiful and be within reasonable distance from manufacturing plant, be high quality and durable, be recyclable after the building life cycle is complete, require a smaller amount of energy than substitute products, the raw material should be versatile and be used to make multiple products if possible and most importantly it must make financial sense or no one will use it.

Industrial hemp meets all of the requirements to become an eco-friendly building material and both the long and short hemp fibers can be used in construction materials. It can be grown organically, it has one of the largest biomass yields in the plant kingdom, can be grown almost anywhere, it's the strongest natural fiber, no mining is needed, it can sequester carbon, preserves soil quality, and it can be used in multiple construction products.

Some construction materials that have incorporated hemp or can be replaced with hemp are plywood, drywall, hemp concrete, hemp fiberboard, office dividers, paints, sealants, carpet, flooring, plaster and insulation batts. To add to that impressive list, University of North Carolina researchers are also trying to develop lumber using hemp fibers and recycled plastic bottles and a Canadian company has made shingles using hemp field scraps.[109]

The most talked about hemp construction material is hemp concrete. It is simply a mixture of hemp hurd fiber (low value part of plant), water, and lime. It is lighter than regular concrete, flame-resistant, mildew resistant, more flexible than conventional concrete and can be used for interior or exterior walls. Hemp concrete is hemp's most common use in European construction. A study done by The Building Research Establishment in England found less energy was consumed constructing a hemp building compared to a conventional building. Less energy consumed means less money wasted during the construction process. The study also found that the finished hemp building had higher thermal inertia and it requires less energy to heat and cool the structure. The drawback of using hemp concrete is that it cannot be used for load bearing support. The most popular use for hemp concrete is applying the product around a timber frame. Hemp concrete is usually applied by using temporary plastic panels that allow the workers to pack the mixture around the wood frame. When the mixture is dry the plastic panels are removed and the result is a watertight building that can sequester carbon and gets stronger throughout its life cycle. Some construction companies have even engineered ways to apply hemp concrete by simply spraying the mixture onto the structure of the building. If you would like to learn more about how to use hemp concrete I suggest checking out one of the numerous hemp construction videos on Youtube.

One of the more talked about hemp structures was created in France and holds 3.5 million bottles of wine. The winery was built using premade 400 mm thick hemp lime panels and was held in space using a steel structure. The hemp construction allowed the wine owner to maintain a constant temperature without using central cooling or heating.[110]

In 2011 Prime Minister of UK David Cameron opened a rural housing complex called Cottsway Housing. Cottsway was made from locally sourced industrial hemp and was part of a Renewable Housing program. Cameron said of the opening, "This development is innovative and creative and Cottsway is leading the way in providing green homes. It is vital to build new housing in rural areas to help sustain local services such as shops and Post Offices." A community school is even being rebuilt with hemp concrete after a fire destroyed parts of the campus. [111]

In the UK a 195,000 sq ft Marks and Spencer store was also just completed using hemp panels. The supplier, Lime Technology produced 230 panels that measure 2.4 m high x 4.8 m wide and 400 mm thick.[112] This store is also the largest M&S store outside of the original flagship store.

Hemp concrete still has areas that can be improved. The lime that is mixed with the hemp hurds requires energy intensive mining and is burned at very high temperatures. Even with the lime calculated into the equation, Lime Technology maintains hemp concrete mixtures can sequester 110 kg of CO_2 per cubic meter. Some experts believe that there needs to be an independent study done and an industry acceptance of what is being measured to accurately attain those results.

When it comes to total life cycle assessments hemp concrete does very well. Breaking the product apart, mixing it with water and adding more lime binder is all that is needed to reuse hemp mixtures. Reusing the material is very important to reduce carbon emissions and make the material more eco-friendly. To adequately improve the sustainability of the construction industry we must focus on replacing concrete with durable and more eco-friendly materials. On a world scale two times as much concrete is produced than steel, aluminum, plastic, and wood combined.[113]

As for other construction materials made from hemp, most of them have a better environmental record than hemp concrete. Hemp insulation for example locks up tons of CO_2 and is one of the most efficient energy saving products on the market. It also can absorb and release moisture to help maintain indoor moisture levels. Hemp insulation is ready to be used by construction companies and has passed all Federal and Municipal fire codes.[114] The product can last as long as the building and if in needs to be disposed of it can just be composted.

Researchers at Stanford University have recently created a synthetic wood using industrial hemp. This biodegradable plastic has the potential to replace a large portion of construction products and is also being looked at for replacing disposable water bottles. Sarah Billington, lead researcher in the report said, "This is a great opportunity to make products that serve a societal need and respect and protect the natural environment." After testing numerous natural materials the group concluded that "the best turned out to be natural hemp fibers fused with a biodegradable plastic resin called polyhdroxy-butyrate (PHB)". Craig Criddle, a professor that was involved said "You can mold it, nail it, hammer it, drill it, a lot like wood. But bioplastic PHB can be produced faster than wood, and hemp can be grown faster than trees."[115]

When it comes to growing industrial crops you can guarantee there will be push back from people claiming industrial crops will raise food prices. This argument however has no basis when discussing hemp construction materials. According to a study done in the UK by Hemp Technology "if industry (housing industry) were to build all the new houses required in the UK (200,000 per year) with Tradical Hemcrete and replace all insulation products with hemp fibre, it would still only require 250,000 hectares of land on which to grow the hemp. This is a small fraction of UK agricultural land." By using hemp concrete to construct houses it could save 30-40% in emissions per house.[116] There is no reason why we shouldn't be able to apply this innovation to the U.S. housing market. The Hemp Technology website also brings up that cereal crops can't be grown without a break crop such as hemp and that hemp is not just an industrial crop when being grown for its seed.[117] In reality if people are concerned about prices going up they should be more worried about what the FED, banking cartel, and the government is doing to devalue our dollar and cause prices to rise.

Hemp Paper

With more individuals and businesses using electronic documents to save paper it is believed that the hemp paper market doesn't have the potential as the previously discussed hemp industries. However, it is a very real possibility that hemp could establish a large niche market in treeless paper products. A niche market that is already established and using hemp paper are cigarette paper manufacturers.

The history of paper could have been completely different if the inventor of the decorticator (hemp processing machine in the early 1900s), George Schlichten would of gotten his way. He spent a large portion of his life dedicated to processing plant fiber for the production of treeless paper. Schlichten believed that in 1917, 50,000 tons of paper could be produced with a price that was 50% of the price of regular newsprint.[118] Consequently, due to the policies that were lobbied by corporate interest we have not been able to make Schlichten's dream a reality. A year before in 1916, USDA Bulletin No. 404 claimed that hemp could produce four times as much fiber per acre over a 20-year period. It should be noted that this statistic was taken before tree farms became popular. The production of hemp paper also could save 75% of the sulfuric acid used to break down the fiber when compared to wood paper and does not require chlorine bleach.

There is not a doubt that the use of tree pulp to create paper is a huge waste of our natural resources, but to realistically replace the entire tree pulp industry hemp would have to be cultivated on a massive scale. Hemp's farm waste would also need to be collected with other cellulosic crops such as flax and straw to help lower prices. Even though this would be difficult, it is definitely possible. Currently it is estimated that hemp paper is over 5 times more expensive than conventional tree paper and is produced in negligible quantities compared to tree paper. This high price can be attributed to the lack of modern technology and investment, which is caused by the lack of a reliable hemp supply. Over the last century investment has catered to developing tree-pulping plants as opposed to plants to process farm fibers. Influential chemical companies and landowners played a major part in this development. If a more sustainable industry is to be created we must begin revamping this technology to allow for the processing of bast fibers.

The environmental benefits of using sustainable agricultural fibers for papermaking are easy to point out. Currently it is estimated that 40% of deforestation worldwide is attributed to the tree pulp and paper industry.[119] Deforestation not only leads to the destruction of priceless habitat for animals and plants, but we loose valuable carbon sinks that are needed to maintain a healthy carbon cycle. The paper industry consumes 4% of all the world's energy (5th biggest consumer) and requires more water per ton produced than any other industry in the world.[120] Natural fibers such as hemp could not only stop the destruction of old forest growth, but also decrease the amount of energy and water needed to produce paper. Hemp has lower lignin content than wood so it needs fewer chemicals to process and can dramatically lower the amount of wastewater created. Hemp also can be recycled up to 8 times, versus only 3 times for wood pulp and does not yellow with age.

The easiest way to fix the problems in the paper industry is to simply stop consuming large quantities of paper. The advancement of technology has allowed us to become more efficient with our paper usage, while also saving us money and time. The implementation of agricultural fibers may be a long-term solution to our paper problem, but powerful lobbyist and a lack of infrastructure will be hard to overcome. In the mean time individuals should stress the importance of recycling the paper that is currently in use. Old newspapers account for the majority of this paper waste, so do the environment and your wallet a favor and get your news online.

Hemp Food & Body Care

"If people let the government decide what foods they eat and what medicines they take, their bodies will soon be in as sorry a state as are the souls who live under tyranny."- Thomas Jefferson

"Let food be thy medicine and medicine be thy food." – Hippocrates

The two most important industries in creating a strong American hemp market are the food and body care industries. These industries are so important because we must establish a strong demand for organic hemp seed in order to give American farmers the economic incentive to grow hemp. Processors of hemp seed can use existing infrastructure, while hemp fiber will need millions of dollars from private investors. As a result, the first hemp crops cultivated in America will focus on hemp seed as opposed to hemp fiber.

As I stated in the preface I am a hemp entrepreneur who is already in the body care industry and has plans to enter the supplement market in 2014. We decided on launching body care and supplement product lines only after researching the characteristics of hemp oil and learning that developing an organic hemp seed market was vital for the American hemp industry. The two industries also work very well together since body care products and supplements are both body enhancers. Many people don't realize that substances you put on your skin will eventually enter your blood stream and what you eat and supplement your diet with plays a huge role on your overall appearance.

Hemp oil and the rest of the natural products we use are carefully selected, but unfortunately I will not be discussing all of my research on hemp oil for liability reasons. Since I am already in the body care industry and plan to enter the supplement industry, it is our understanding the Federal Trade Commission does not allow us to restate any medical studies or benefits regarding hemp oil, hemp foods, or natural products. Doing so would reclassify my cosmetics or supplements as a "drug," which would cost millions of dollars to get approved for market. In my opinion these laws are a blatant violation of the first amendment that guarantees our freedom of free speech. If my company were to market any studies of hemp oil or even put testimonial on our website claiming any benefits we would risk having our business shut down by armed federal agents. In recent years the Feds have increased their raids on natural supplement suppliers as well as raw food producers across the nation. This is a very fine line and Instead of risking prosecution I have chosen to not discuss this section in detail.

"Congress shall make no law respecting an establishment of religion, or prohibiting the free exercise thereof; or abridging the freedom of speech, or of the press; or the right of the people peaceably to assemble, and to petition the Government for a redress of grievances." – First amendment

It is no secret that we are what we eat and our bodies are works of art that are derived from the foods we consume. It is also no secret that our current subsidized food system is over producing foods that make us unhealthy and sick. To top all this off the Feds won't allow food and supplement companies to market the healthy aspects of their products without having to worry about repercussions. These policies are only successful at creating a broken food industry that is more worried about profit than health. Under current regulations the Feds are actually in the business of protecting pharmaceutical monopolies instead of protecting the consumer. The ability to punish supplement and cosmetic manufacturers for making health claims gives the drug industry a government assisted monopoly on curing all diseases. By keeping food and supplement benefits as far away from the public's eye as possible, the pharmaceutical industry has kept many people in the dark about the importance of nutrition. The FDA regulations clearly state a drug is the only thing that can cure a disease and the pharmaceutical industries goal is to get everything classified as a disease. By classifying everything as a disease this will mean only drugs can make medical statements and it will help keep small competitors from entering the marketplace. The result is a decrease in competition and a decline in our health choices. These federal regulations also give the health industry the incentive to only create products that cure diseases as opposed to preventative medicine.

Even though the government has suppressed my freedom of speech, they cannot deter our customers and potential customers from doing a quick online search regarding hemp foods and cosmetics. Readers can find the true benefits of hemp by looking for third party literature. I will only claim that hemp has an amazing nutritional profile that according to Hemp Oil Canada includes folate (B9, thiamine (vitamin B1), riboflavin (vitamin B2), niacin (vitamin B3), vitamin B6, vitamin E. potassium, calcium, iron, phosphorous, magnesium, copper, zinc and Omegas 3,6, and 9. One of the great aspects of hemp oil is its 3:1 ratio of omega 6 to omega 3. Many researchers have claimed that this 3:1 ratio is perfect for the human diet and that the American omega 6 to omega 3 ratio is way too high (Closer to 15:1 – 25:1). Hemp seeds are also considered a complete protein and contain all the essential amino & fatty acids your body needs

People that choose to supplement their diets with hemp products or use hemp body care products also do not have to worry about failing any drug tests that test for THC. North American hemp food processors pledge to make sure all of their products contain negligible quantities of THC and hemp will not cause users to fail drug tests. To learn more about the pledge please visit TestPledge.com.

There is a major problem in our health care and agriculture systems today and they both need fundamental changes if we are going to become a more prosperous and healthy nation. Currently 68% of the population is overweight and over a third of the population is obese. America's obesity has created trillions of dollars in medical expenses and this is a direct result of the lack of healthy alternatives in both medicine and agriculture. Government subsidization of processed foods that knowingly create health problems is also one of the most idiotic and unethical practices in the world.

HempStrong hopes to have self-educated customers when it comes to health and sustainability and we look forward to you spreading the word about our products and all that hemp has to offer. I hope my readers can take a break here and do some of their own research on hemp's nutritional profile and its characteristics. If you are feeling bold you should do some added research on the war against natural supplements and how the human *endocannabinoid system* can benefit from hemp oil. Every human is born with an endocannabinoid system that can utilize the cannabinoids that are present in the cannabis sativa family of plants. Cannabinoids levels are much higher in cannabis that is cultivated for medical marijuana, but cannabinoids show tremendous promise and should be given every chance to compete with traditional medicines. The U.S. government even holds a patent that deals with cannabinoids and their health benefits.

Hemp Farming

"All truth comes from nature." – Himalayan nomad saying

As previously stated industrial hemp is thought to be one of the first cultivated crops in the world. People need to realize however that just legalizing industrial hemp will not create a prosperous industry. To create a thriving hemp industry that could compete with China all stakeholders must be united. Stakeholders include public servants, law enforcement, regulators, farmers, processors, businesses, and consumers. All of these stakeholders must work together and upon legalization of industrial hemp we must make sure that farmers benefit from growing the crop. Without willing farmers the manufacturers won't have the opportunity to utilize the plant and consumers will never have an opportunity to buy home grown hemp products.

In the 18th century farmers in Kentucky began growing

hemp for textiles, but they soon found it had tremendous benefits for their soil. Hemp's greatest asset for farmers is not creating paper wealth, but giving back to their land. As FDR famously said "the nation that destroys its soil destroys itself."

Hemp is perfect for crop rotation and it is recommended that farmers have a rotation of four crops including industrial hemp. It has been shown that farmers could grow consecutive years of industrial hemp without seeing much difference in total yield, but this can increase the chance of diseases. Some farmers in Kentucky reported growing hemp over 10 years in a row without seeing any change in yields. In Canada it is grown both with the fertilizers nitrogen, phosphorus, and potassium as well as organically. Although organic hemp farmers see a lower yield, they tend to see the same amount of return since the higher prices for organic hemp seeds make up for the lower yield. To go along with being a great crop for rotational purposes hemp has also been shown to remove heavy metals and toxins from the soil. The process of removing heavy metals and toxins through the use of plants is called Phytoremediation and hemp is one of the plant kingdoms highest performers. It has been planted at toxic waste sites throughout the world, including nuclear disaster sites such as Chernobyl.

Even when grown with added agrochemicals hemp still requires fewer chemicals than the leading mono-crops in America and leaves around 50% of these nutrients in the field for the proceeding crop. Nitrogen is the most environmentally damaging nutrient out of the three chemicals and farmers should be cautious about over applying nitrogen to hemp crops since it leads to lower quality fibers. By decreasing the amount of agrochemicals used we will begin to see an improvement in aquatic eco-systems across America.

Farm pollution is one of the leading causes of damage to eco-systems and it is the root cause of the growing "dead zone" in the Gulf of Mexico. This is a problem that not only boat captains in the Gulf of Mexico want solved, but environmentalist and fishermen throughout the globe are worried about the environmental devastation that is caused by farm runoff. The question is how do we fix this problem?

Many policy makers in Washington are attempting to push more regulations onto the farmers, but do we really want to be making it harder for the men & women who put food on our table? And what would be the unintended consequences and costs of implementing more regulation in the market? Higher food prices and small farmers getting out of the business due to high regulatory costs could be real possibilities of more regulation. This is the exact opposite of what America needs; we need more small organic farmers and lower prices for nutritious whole foods. This will not only help our environment and rural economy, but also improve our health. To overhaul our farming practices we simply need to empower the small farmer and stop giving government handouts to corporate farmers. Current farming practices today are only succeeding in subsidizing our unhealthy addiction to processed foods and subsidizing the destruction of our environment.

Farmers and state officials in Iowa have proposed a water quality plan of action in hopes of preventing any future regulations. The proposal is only voluntary right now, but experts believe that if changes in water quality are not seen soon, regulation will be coming in the very near future. The two nutrients that are the focus of the proposal are nitrogen and phosphorus. Nitrogen is usually washed directly into waterways, while phosphorus usually stays with the soil and is washed into waterways through erosion.[121] Industrial hemp could help improve water quality by strategically planting hemp in areas where farm runoff is most prominent. The hemp crops would help uptake and filter a large portion of the nitrogen and since hemp can be cultivated using no till practices it could help prevent soil erosion. The goal of the Iowa proposal is to reduce the amount of nitrogen and phosphorus that is finding its way into the Gulf by 45%.[122] The hawkeye state should do themselves and our environment a favor and take a lead role in legalizing industrial hemp.

The nitrogen and phosphorous that finds its way into the Mississippi River is eventually deposited in the Gulf of Mexico where it encourages the growth of dangerous algae blooms. When the algae blooms begin to die and decompose this depletes oxygen levels in the water and the aquatic species that do not vacate the area begin to die, hence the name "dead zone."

Hemp's ability to be grown organically while having minimal pest problems is very rare in American agriculture. In the future hemp will be essential in creating a healthier and more sustainable farming industry. Hemp can also be utilized as a natural companion crop to the rest of the plants in cultivation. Studies have shown that damages from pests have been far lower on crops that are planted near industrial hemp fields.

In order to cultivate industrial hemp in Canada farmers must meet a series of requirements and are only allowed to plant approved hemp strains that are regulated by Health Canada. These strains of hemp contain THC levels of 0.3% or lower and they have even bred a strain in France that has no THC in it at all.

For best yields hemp should be planted in soil that has a pH above 6 and be on well-drained land. To much moisture in the soil could stunt the growth of hemp plants and cause weaker stalks that can't support the weight of the seeds. According to Ridgetown College, hemp needs as little as 10-13 inches of rainfall during the growing season.[123] This low amount of water compared to alternative crops can be attributed to the high density of the plant that shades the soil and reduces the amount of water lost through evaporation. Hemp also establishes a long taproot that allows it to reach water where other plants cannot. During drought seasons hemp has a much better chance of producing a consistent yield than competing crops.

The planting of industrial hemp occurs in the spring and farmers have the option of either planting hemp for fiber, seed, or a dual purpose. As the hemp industry develops it is expected that planting hemp for dual purposes will be less and less popular as farmers will start breeding seeds that create uniform fiber lengths or produce large quantities of seed. Hemp can either be monoecious, meaning both male and female parts are on the same plant or dioecious, meaning male and female plants are separate.

A big concern for law enforcement is the possibility of marijuana growers growing their female plants near or in hemp fields. This is a valid concern, but marijuana growers would actually go out of business if they decided to grow their female plants next to a hemp fields. This is due to the wind pollination that would come from the strains of hemp. If a marijuana grower planted pot plants with 10% THC next to a hemp field the THC level would end up getting diluted due to the wind pollination, thus creating inferior marijuana. Industrial hemp is also harvested before marijuana plants are fully developed. If somebody would have the stupidity to plant marijuana in a field that the police already have the GPS coordinates to they would have to cut around their marijuana plants while harvesting hemp. This would thus make it easier for law enforcement to notice the left over marijuana plants from the air.

Even though hemp is pest resilient it does have its fair share of pests and diseases that farmers should be looking out for. Botrytis cinerea and Sclerotinia sclerotiorum are two molds that have been seen on hemp crops in Canada and hemp is also susceptible to grasshoppers, corn borer, birds, and bertha army worm to name a few.[124]

If the farmer is growing hemp for fiber it usually takes around 90 days until the plant is ready for harvest and 125 days if the hemp is being grown for seed. During the development of the hemp industry in Canada and Europe farmers had a problem getting the right type of machinery to harvest their crops and the strong hemp fibers would often cause damages to the modified machinery. In recent years technological breakthroughs have led to more efficient and durable harvesting equipment. In some parts of Asia and Eastern Europe hemp is still harvested in the traditional way by hand.

Hemp grown for seed and hemp grown for fiber are harvested in two different ways, but they can both be harvested using the same equipment. Hemp seed is usually harvested at a higher height, while hemp fiber is often cut near the base of he plant. The traditional way of harvesting hemp was to lay the hemp fiber in the field where it begins the process of dew retting. Dew retting is the microbial process where nature's elements help to break apart the bonds that hold together the hurds and fibers. Dew retting allows for easier processing of the plant and has been used for centuries. There are also two other retting processes called water retting and machine retting. Once the hemp stalks are cut and are laying on the field the dew retting process takes 3-4 weeks to complete depending on the weather conditions. During this time the stalks are turned midway to ensure there is consistent retting. During the turning of the stalks is when many of the leaves are knocked off the plant and return their nutrients to the soil. After the retting period is finished the hemp stalks are baled and prepared for dry storage. It is important that the moisture content of the stalks is no more than 15% or the fibers may become rotted during storage. Hemp bales are best stored indoors where moisture can't damage the yield.

To go along with being a profitable crop that has tremendous benefits for the soil and the environment, hemp can also serve as animal feed and animal bedding on the farm. Hemp animal feed is called hemp cake and is made from the hemp seeds after they have been crushed for their oils. Hemp animal feed has been show to be an adequate replacement for corn and soy meal and some animals can benefit tremendously from its nutritional profile and high amount of essential fatty acids. Hemp animal bedding is made from the stem of the plant and is highly absorbent. Farmers that have switched to hemp bedding use less bedding and have smaller labor costs. Queen Elizabeth even uses hemp bedding for her royal horses. The same byproduct used for animal bedding has also been found to be useful on bird farms where bird manure creates toxic runoffs. Traditionally wood chips have been used to catch bird waste, but this creates a mess that leads to environmental problems. Industrial hemp could help clean up these messy systems and create more ethical living conditions for the animals.

A recent hemp innovation on the farm has come from a farm machinery manufacturer in Canada called Buhler Industries. They hope to make farming more sustainable by using hemp fiber to create tractor parts. Just think of a world where crops are harvested by tractors made from hemp fiber and powered by hemp bio-fuel.

How Much Do Farmers Make Growing Hemp?

Farmer's that choose to grow industrial hemp at the very least can expect to see an increase in the quality of their soil and many farmers have seen an increase in the following crops yield. These two benefits alone should be very appealing to farmers, but when it comes down to it farmers are only going to grow hemp if it makes economic sense.

Upon legalization farmers will most likely be forced into buying certified seed since the THC content of the seeds will concern regulators. Keeping good control of the seeds will be a vital part of maintaining a respectable hemp industry, but farmers must make sure they do not allow seed monopolies to control the market. As the hemp industry begins to flourish farmers should expect to see higher yields due to an increase in seed breeding and an improvement in their soil. The first hemp crops that will be grown in the United States will most likely be grown from imported Canadian seed. The most common strands are Alyssa, Anka, CRS-1, CFX-1, CFX-2,

Delores and Finola.

Since hemp farmers will have to depend on seed yields during the early years of the American hemp industry, knowing how much money hemp seeds can bring to the farmers table is essential. The record for seed yield in Canada has been 2000 lbs per acre, but a farmer can expect on average anywhere from 600-800 lbs and this number is steadily increasing. According to the Manitoba Agriculture, Food and Rural Initiatives in Canada the price for clean seed ranges from $0.75 to $0.90 per pound and Organic seed is usually 30 to 40% higher.

Estimates from Manitoba Canada in January 2013 found hemp oil could have a profit margin of 10.7%, and have an operating expense ratio of 54.6%. Hemp farmer Reuben Stone has reported an average return of $290 per acre and this doesn't even include the hemp fiber.[125]

All farmers that plan on growing hemp seed should plan on getting a guaranteed contract with a processor before growing!

How Hemp Can Help Reclaim Mt. Top Removal Sites?

In one of the previous sections you read that hemp biomass could be burned similar to coal or even with coal to reduce emissions. A company called Patriot Bioenergy Corporation is looking to do just that in Kentucky and even plans to experiment with growing hemp on abandoned mountain top removal sites all across the Appalachians. This could improve the environment as well as give areas of high unemployment more job opportunities.

After a mountain is blasted the majority of the land is left undeveloped and in Kentucky and West Virginia only around 4% of the previous mining sites have any economic activity. When the miners leave they are required to lay down a thin layer of soil that is highly acidic and has a hard time supporting native species. This overburden soil contributes to flash floods, landslides, has a high amount of heavy metals and clogs waterways. Many have hopes that hemp's characteristics can have tremendous benefits to improving soil quality and preventing future flash floods. The idea is that after planting multiple years of hemp the soil will be in a better position to nourish native plant species. The people who call these areas home also need the jobs that a new hemp industry could provide. The majority of counties that mine coal have higher poverty rates and an increase in health problems when compared to surrounding counties. Legalizing hemp could go along way in helping to transform their rural economies. Not legalizing industrial hemp is a vote for the status quo and a vote against job opportunities.

Hemp Internationally

Thanks in large part to the Internet, more and more people are becoming aware of the many benefits of industrial hemp. Currently leaders in the United States are either unaware, in deep denial, or being lobbied by interest groups to keep industrial hemp classified as a narcotic drug similar to crack, cocaine, and heroin. In 1961 the United Nations paved the way for the reintroduction of industrial hemp for those countries that permitted it. More recently both the NAFTA and GATT international trade agreements acknowledged that hemp was an important agricultural crop. After reading up to this point I know all of my readers now know industrial hemp is far from being a dangerous drug and so do the men and women in the following countries.

Australia:

In 1994 the Australian government revitalized the hemp industry by allowing their first test plot to be grown and commercial licenses have been granted in the state of Victoria since 1998. Other Australian states would join the hemp movement in the following years. Currently one of the main emphasis on Australia's infant hemp industry is the use of hemp materials in construction. In a country where 54% of the landmass is in the hands of farmers, hemp could have a big impact if accepted on a larger scale.

Austria:

Industrial hemp was never prohibited in Austria. Austrian hemp entrepreneurs specialize in making hemp foods, body care products, beer, and they were the first European country to make hemp milk from the hemp seeds. Austrians also specialize in using a substance called hempstone that is used to manufacture musical instruments, furniture and musical speakers. The amazing thing is hempstone is made only using hemp fibers and water, no additives or glues needed.

Canada:

Canadians began cultivating industrial hemp test plots in 1994 and by 1998 they had their first full growing season. Health Canada is responsible for regulating the industry and law enforcement has had no problem with farmers planting marijuana plants in their hemp fields.

Chile:

Hemp has been grown in all regions of Chile, but by the 1980s hemp was being grown only in the central regions and was on the decline due to synthetic alternatives for ropes and sacks.[126] Today hemp remains legal, but is just cultivated for a small niche market. It has been reported the Chile has shown interest in building up their hemp industry. It should be noted here that throughout Latin America both hemp and marijuana have different names for medicinal consumption.[127]

China:

According to the founder of EnviroTextiles; Barbara Filippone, "No other country's fabric can match the integrity of Chinese hemp."[128] Over the last few decades China has been liberalizing their economy and with more freedom came the reemergence of the industrial hemp industry. In 1987 the first modern hemp mill was opened in the Tai'an district of Dong Ping and by 1993 they had attracted outside investors from the Netherlands. Today China is proud to say they have the largest hemp production facility in the world that employs 2,600 workers and is capable of producing 3.6 million yards of hemp cloth.[129]

Denmark:

The revitalization of the Denmark hemp industry occurred in 1997 and the farmers there are committed to using strictly organic cultivation methods. In 2012 VIA University College in Horsens, Denmark published a study titled *Is Hemp A Sustainable Construction Material.* The study found hempcrete is not completely sustainable because the lime or clay binders used are not renewable, but "hempcrete fulfills all other points for eco-friendliness and hides great potential in the attempt of reducing carbon emissions." The study also found that all soil nutrients should be natural, the hemp industry should be decentralized and processed as locally as possible, and hemp should be farmed using machinery running off hemp biofuels.

Finland:

Hemp seeds in Finland have been found dating back to A.D. 1000 and believed to have come from Russia.[130] Similar to many countries throughout Europe the Finns lost interest in the plant after WWII even though it was never prohibited. The decline was contributed to the globalization of agriculture and the replacement of hemp and flax textiles with cheaper cotton imports. The Finns financed a large portion of their cotton imports by cutting down their forests. The resurgence of the hemp industry occurred in 1995 with the development of FINOLA, a variety of hemp that produces both fiber and seeds.

France:

France isn't just known for its wines and champagnes. It has been growing hemp for over 600 years and is one of Europe's biggest producers. In 2011 France cultivated just over 27,000 acres, which was used to make specialty papers, plastics in automotives, construction materials and high quality animal bedding.

Germany:

Germany prohibited the cultivation of industrial hemp beginning in 1982, but just over a decade later they began research to bring the crop back into production. In 1995 hemp was once again legal to grow in Germany. Germany also plays host to the annual International Conference of the

European Industrial Hemp Association, which is known as the largest meeting of hemp stakeholders in the world.

Hungary:

During the time Hungary was locked into the Soviet bloc it was the Soviet Union's number one supplier of hemp products. Now Hungary specializes in an assortment of rugs, textiles, and fabrics, while also exporting hemp seed and fiberboard for construction. Hungary benefits from cheap labor, but is lacking the investment to take its hemp industry to the next level. Hungary's varieties of hemp are known throughout the hemp industry as having the highest yields of both fiber and seed.

Japan:

Japan has a long history of cultivating industrial hemp and was one of the first regions to make paper and clothes from the long fibers. The Japanese Emperors even wore special hemp clothing for ceremonies . After WWII, the U.S. along with our allies forced the Japanese to pass the Hemp Control Act. Ironically going to war with Japan forced United States to grow industrial hemp for the war efforts, but when the war ended they halted the cultivation in Japan. The effort to re-legalize industrial hemp that began in the 1970s went hand in hand with the movement to rid American military presence from their country. Many of the finest and most important garments in the Japanese cultural utilize industrial hemp including the thong of Zouri (Sandals), robes for religious and political leaders and loincloths that Sumo wrestlers sport. Hemp is a vital part of Japanese cultural and many of the hemp licenses are given to farmers practicing Nara sarashi, which involves hemp weaving.

Netherlands:

Industrial hemp was reintroduced in the Netherlands in 1993 with the help of Dutch entrepreneur Ben Dronkers. He started the company HempFlax and in the first full growing season HempFlax grew 343 acres. HempFlax not only started the hemp movement in the Netherlands, but invented new hemp harvesting equipment, and improved processing methods.

New Zealand:

New Zealand was given the opportunity to grow industrial hemp in 2006 and uses no subsidies in its agriculture program. Hemp regulation is very similar to Canadian laws.

Poland:

Poland began breeding hemp plants in 1946 and in 2008 they cultivated just under 4,000 acres. The Polish hemp industry is regulated by the Drugs Act of July 29,2005 and requires hemp to have less than 0.2% THC.

Romania:

Romania was another country that was a large supplier to the Soviet Bloc until it broke apart. Hemp runs deep in the history of this area and many of the processing techniques in place today are the same methods used hundreds of years ago. Romania is consistently producing large quantities of industrial hemp every year and is a great example of a country that could see a big improvement in the hemp industry with more outside investment. Romania's most important asset is it's fertile soil for growing organic hemp.

Spain:

Spain has never prohibited the cultivation of industrial hemp and throughout their history they have specialized in creating specialty papers and textiles.

South Africa:

The hemp movement in South Africa has been revitalized in recent years with the help of hard working entrepreneurs. Currently hemp can only be grown for research purposes, but the importation of hemp products and the construction of the first hemp house in South Africa have gone a long way in bringing awareness to the plant. South African hemp farmers biggest hurdle may lay in the United States as government officials are weary of legalizing industrial hemp in fear they could lose aid from the United States and thus political support.

Switzerland:

Is home to the CannaTrade international hemp fair and one of the leading European suppliers of hemp construction material.

United Kingdom:

The farmers within the United Kingdom were prohibited from growing industrial hemp starting in 1971 (most likely because of pressure from business interests within the United States), but in 1993 prohibition was lifted and ever since the government has been encouraging a natural fibers industry with hemp. The government has been very supportive of the industry by giving subsidies to farmers and guaranteeing grants to companies. When hemp is legalized in the United States farmers should not expect to receive any government handouts.

Global Effort

These are just some of the countries that allow growing industrial hemp. Others include Egypt, Slovenia, South Korea, Ukraine and Yugoslavia. Many countries choose not to grow industrial hemp simply because of American laws and the influence of foreign aid. With the renewed interest in the sustainability of industrial hemp we must change our policies in America so we can help lead the way for the rest of the world.

Closer Look At Canada

After 50 years of industrial hemp prohibition, Canada legalized industrial hemp in 1998. In 1994, Canadian government officials allowed research plots to be studied in hopes of finding the best plant varieties and market potential of industrial hemp. Many universities, private companies, and government organization took advantage of these licenses. It was the work of these academic universities and corporations that eventually pushed the Canadian government to legalize industrial hemp in 1998. This is one of the main factors keeping the DEA from granting any licenses to study industrial hemp. They know from looking at Canada that once the universities and private sector start clamoring about the benefits of industrial hemp, legalization is soon to come.

"All truths are easy to understand once they are discovered; the point is to discover them." - Galileo Galilei

An organization called Health Canada was given the responsibility of regulating the cultivation of the first crops in 1998. These regulations were strict and drew a fine line between industrial hemp and other forms of cannabis. Under the new regulations, industrial hemp was listed as a plant that is a member of the cannabis sativa family that has less than 0.3 percent THC. Health Canada also created a document called The Industrial Hemp Technical Manual that was given to farmers and law enforcement officers assigned to analyze industrial hemp samples. Currently industrial hemp is still not listed as a major crop in Canada, but it is a rapidly growing industry. The consumers that are pushing this industry along and providing the biggest export market to the Canadian hemp farmers reside south of the boarder in America. An Agriculture and Agri-Foods Canada report suggested that nearly 60 percent of hemp exports from Canada end up in America. The statement that Health Canada gave for legalizing and regulating industrial hemp goes as followed:

"In recent years, interest in the cultivation of industrial hemp, as a potential source of new jobs, has grown in the agricultural and industrial sectors, as has the need for the development of alternative sources of fibre. In addition, the information gathered as a result of the issuance of research licenses over the past four years has indicated that industrial hemp could be successfully grown in Canada as a separate entity from Cannabis (marihuana). With such a demand and the encouraging research findings, Health Canada chose to give the agricultural and industrial sectors the opportunity to build what is essentially a new industry by changing the laws restricting the cultivation of industrial hemp."[131]

For those who wish to get into the industrial hemp business, whether growing or processing, they must have a valid license from Health Canada. Each applicant must submit their basic information plus the location of where industrial hemp is to be stored, sold, cultivated, the amount of acres to be cultivated for seed and fiber, Global Positioning System (GPS) location of hemp field, and proof of land ownership. Farmers who wish to grow seed are required to be members of the Canadian Seed Growers Association. The facilities that are used to test the varieties of industrial hemp for THC content must also apply for a license through Health Canada. If an applicant meets all these requirements and can pass a ten year background check they are granted a license to grow industrial hemp. Upon receiving their license, the farmers may only grow the variety of hemp that they applied to grow and they must submit samples to licensed testing laboratories to check for THC content at their cost. The licenses given out by Health Canada are only valid for one year and farmers must renew annually if they wish to continue growing industrial hemp. Farmers must also keep an accurate log of harvest information and include where the raw material is sold. If any farmer or processor miss handles or violates any laws outline in the Industrial Hemp Technical Manual there are harsh penalties that include revoking license, cancelation of application, denial of future licenses, and having to deal with the authorities.

One of the biggest hurdles Americans face in their fight to legalize industrial hemp is building the proper regulatory infrastructure. This will take the cooperation of both state and federal governments and a large amount of time and investment. In the 1990s the Canadian officials were able to work closely with private businesses in an effort to get this done in a meaningful and efficient fashion. To be successful in legalizing industrial hemp Americans are going to have to get the same cooperation from our elected officials. States that are leading the push for industrial hemp must be prepared to either provide the necessary funds to set up this regulatory program and lab testing or begin looking for partners to privatize the testing of industrial hemp. By privatizing the testing of THC content governments will save money up front and enterprises will bid competitively for state contracts. The private laboratories would then work directly with local law enforcement to verify the THC content of their local crops. Currently THC content can be tested using a gas chromatography or high performance liquid chromatography. By privatizing the industry we will also be empowering entrepreneurs to invest in more efficient and more cost effective ways to measure THC content. Entrepreneurs that are successful at lowering the costs will thus be rewarded with more state and local contracts. Gas chromatography machines can also already be found in many police stations and forensic science units. Health Canada has even excluded certain varieties of industrial hemp from being tested in laboratories due to there past record of having minimal THC.

The biggest concern about industrial hemp legalization is the idea that marijuana plants (high in THC) would find there way into industrial hemp fields. Many members in the DEA and other law enforcement agencies in the United States support this claim, but this has been a non-issue in Canada according to the Royal Mounted Canadian Police (RMCP). In a Minnesota Department of Agriculture report in 2010, the RMCP were questioned about any marijuana activity in hemp fields. The RMCP claimed that due to the biological makeup of the two plants, marijuana growers stayed far away from industrial hemp farms fearing that the cross-pollination would contaminate and lower their own THC content. They went on to say that because of two different harvesting seasons for industrial hemp and marijuana (marijuana taking longer to develop) it did not make sense for the two plants to share the same field.

Chapter 4: HempStrong

"We do not inherit the Earth from our ancestors, we borrow it from our children." - Native American proverb (Chief Seattle)

"Big business depends entirely on the patronage of those who buy its products: the biggest enterprises loses its power and its influence when it loses its customers." - Ludwig Von Mises

As I've already mentioned I am an entrepreneur and co-founder of HempStrong Brands. HempStrong hopes to be a trailblazer in the industrial hemp movement by creating high quality branded hemp products that improve the lives of our customers as well as our environment.

I believe the entrepreneurship bug bit me at an early age. The most memorable lesson I remember receiving was in elementary school when I was given the opportunity to create and run whatever business I wanted for an entire week. We used fake monopoly money with our teacher's faces on them and we were able to make partnership agreements with our fellow classmates. In essence my teachers developed a mini economy. I believe the whole week was financed by local businesses and I was lucky enough to take part in this when I was in the 3rd and 5th grade. Leading up to entrepreneurship week we had to write out our business idea and at the start of the week we were giving X amount of dollars and told to make it last. At the end of each day we balanced the books and recorded our profit (or loss). Even in elementary school our teachers didn't bail out any unsuccessful businesses and luckily we didn't have any taxes.

I remember my business in 3rd grade was a called SA Sport Center (for Scott & Aaron). For $5 my partner and I would let our friends come use all the recess equipment for 30 minutes. I know what you're thinking... Genius! My partner and I were meeting the demand of every elementary student in the building. Lets just say those were the glory years, making money was as easy as letting my friends go play. During these entrepreneurship weeks I learned that the market worked and I owe this lesson to my 3rd, 4th, and 5th grade teachers.

Throughout my college career I had a passion for big projects and becoming an entrepreneur. Consequently, by the end of my sophomore year I had stopped listening to what my teachers were saying and would spend most my time reading any entrepreneurial book I could get my hands on. My junior year I even dropped out for a semester to start a shoe company and learn more about entrepreneurship. Sadly my shoe company failed to launch and I ended up going back to school the next semester, but I had learned more during that one semester than the rest of my college career combined.

The great thing about growing up in the information age is that you don't need to go to college to get educated. All you need is Internet access and you can learn anything your heart desires. For me I learned everything I could about starting a small business. I followed blogs, read thousands of articles, followed my favorite businesses and entrepreneurs and occasionally paid $10 bucks to download an eBook onto my Mac. The entrepreneurs that influenced me the most were Richard Branson (Virgin), Yvon Chouinard (Patagonia), Paul Hawken (writer/entrepreneur), Timothy Ferris (Author of the 4 Hour Work Week), Blake Mycoskie (Toms), and of course Steve Jobs (Apple).

I got involved in the hemp industry after I learned about hemp clothing while working on an apparel venture in college. I soon found that hemp had a lot of potential in the natural fiber and food markets and would be worth pursuing. I also discovered that the city I lived in during college, Lexington Kentucky, use to be the center of the American hemp trade during the 19th century. After learning about how the hemp industry reestablished itself in Canada I partnered with my original co-founder Michael Bumgarner and we would soon settle on introducing a body care and supplement company under the HempStrong family of brands.

We decided to focus on the body care and supplement industries since they specialized in utilizing the nutritious hemp oil. In order to grow the hemp industry upon legalization we realized that we must have the hemp seed (hemp oil) market as developed as possible. A more developed market will give farmers a bigger incentive to grow the plant. Currently all of our products under the HempStrong family of brands use hemp materials imported from Canada. In a few years we envision our raw materials will be grown on American farms all across the nation.

During the months it took to write this book and create the HempStrong identity I was also learning about the sustainability of the world's supply chains, or lack thereof. I found that there was a lot of damage being done by businesses, but instead of looking at businesses and capitalism as the root problem I decided to look at them as part of the solution. Businesses have the power to adapt to changing markets faster than any regulation and entrepreneurs have the knowledge to create the innovation needed to build a more sustainable supply chain. I founded HempStrong with this in mind and our goal is to create a more sustainable and healthier planet.

Views

"Sometimes the questions are complicated and the answers are simple." – Dr. Seuss

We believe the best way to go about legalizing industrial hemp is to build businesses that implement change and let consumers do the voting. Our company believes there is a real problem in the way many products are made in the United States and we could take a step in the right direction by legalizing industrial hemp.

Our focus will be on revamping consumer products at the design stage to eliminate waste, utilize more sustainable materials, and create healthier products. Roughly 90% of a products eco-footprint is created during the important design stage and this is what we will focus on. From lip balms to surfboards more than 25,000 consumer products could be made more sustainable and or healthier with all natural hemp.

Our first project is a body care company called *Hemp & Honey Plus* (powered by HempStrong), but we hope to build upon the HempStrong brand & launch new products in whatever industry we see fit. We believe that hemp can once again become one of the most traded commodities on Earth and HempStrong hopes to help pave the way.

HempStrong's team enjoys spending time outdoors and cleaning up the environment is a big part of this company's purpose. We believe everything is connected through nature and that fixing our environment, health, and economic problems as a nation can be done simultaneously.

Environmental vision

"The way we treat rivers reflects the way we treat each other."
- Aldo Leopold

Worldwide our rivers are constantly being polluted by urban developments and manufacturing plants, yet the biggest culprits are large commercial farms. This pollution is causing problems throughout the food chain and many of these developments are going unseen. HempStrong believes this is a huge problem and it all starts with our unsustainable supply chains. All life on earth depends on water and we can't afford to be polluting our most sacred resource anymore.

One of the biggest problems we hope to alleviate is the fresh water shortage happening not only in America, but all across the world. To tackle this problem we must begin to use water more efficiently and stop polluting the water we have. As you've already learned hemp requires little water when compared to other food and fiber crops and can easily be grown organically. These two characteristics make hemp very beneficial to grow, not only to improve water quality, but water quantity as well.

Some environmentalists shun the idea of using economic incentives or markets to bring about positive benefits for the environment, but the results don't lie. The proper economic incentives can influence landowners to use less agrochemicals, grow more trees, and even improve habitat for endangered animals. The study of both economics and ecology are very similar in the regards that one focuses on how individuals freely interact to create prosperity and the other focuses on how organisms and species freely interact to increase biodiversity. We believe to become economically stable we must become more environmentally sustainable and vice versa. In order to accomplish both of these goals we need to stop supporting economic policies that subsidize pollution, distort markets and encourage waste. Many times markets are wrongly blamed for environmental problems, when in actuality the environmental problem exists because markets are not allowed to function properly and private property laws are not being enforced. The prohibition of hemp and the failure to establish efficient water markets are two perfect examples of markets not being allowed to function properly. The result is a downgrade in environmental quality.

According the United States Department of Agriculture (USDA), agriculture accounts for roughly 80% of the country's water consumed per year and in some western states it is closer to 90%.[132] This figure is far to high and as a result we are drying up rivers and streams, as well as depleting precious groundwater reserves. To top this off it is estimated that 70% of the water taken for agriculture purposes doesn't even reach the crop due to poor engineering, leaky irrigation and evaporation.[133] As for the rest of the water that humans consume, about 2/3rds of the water is used in manufacturing and the rest is used for domestic reasons. What this tells us is that the most efficient way we can make an impact on our water footprint is changing what we farm and how we farm it. By changing what we grow we can begin to change how we manufacturer. Installing water efficient appliances and replacing your old showerhead with a low flow showerhead might make you feel all warm and fuzzy inside, but in reality this will not lower our water footprint in any meaningful way. We must attack this problem from the supply chain as opposed to regulating the amount of water coming out of a showerhead. Don't get me wrong; installing more water efficient devices is a good thing, but its not going to fix the problem. HempStrong wants to see real results as opposed to feeling that warm and fuzzy feeling inside and this means we must fix our water footprint starting with how we grow our food and raw materials.

Most people only drink a couple liters of liquids a day and have very little idea how much water they actually consume. Everything has a water cost and we believe that if people better understood their own water footprint and their products water footprint it could change the world. We envision a future just around the corner where businesses emphasize the importance of water conservation as much as energy conservation. To better understand your own water footprint you can go to waterfootprints.org and use their free online calculator.

HempStrong believes that it is only a matter of time before the global water crisis becomes a mainstream issue. The bottom line is that we must begin to utilize our water resources much more efficiently if we plan on maintaining our high standard of living. As the population expands and more people demand water intensive foods and products, the market price of water will continually increase. It is important that we begin to establish water markets so entrepreneurs and inventors can begin planning for our future. If we plan on having an adequate supply of water entrepreneurs must know at what price water desalinization makes more sense than groundwater pumping or diverting water from rivers. Market prices are the only way stakeholders can receive this valuable information.

After diving into the causes of our global problem we believe the most effective way to curve our water usage is decentralizing the agriculture industry and rewarding farmers for saving water. This will create an atmosphere that encourages efficiency and competition, shows the true cost of water and rewards new water saving technologies. A 2009 study done by the World Bank stated that current agriculture practices that are dominated by monoculture, agrochemicals, and subsidized water prices would need a "transformational overhaul." We believe it is our business's responsibility to partake and influence this transformation. By changing America's farming habits we can influence the world, no red tape needed.

The President's advisors even agree with the need to overhaul American farming. A recent report to the president claimed the top priorities should be "The need to manage new pests, pathogens, and invasive plants; increase the efficiency of water use; reduce the environmental footprint of agriculture; adapt to a changing climate; and accommodate demands for bioenergy—all while continuing to produce safe and nutritious food at home and for those in need abroad."[134] Hemp could be beneficial in improving all of these needs.

Daniel Schrag, co-chair of the President's Council of Advisors on Science and Technology (PCAST), Agricultural Preparedness Working Group said, "Meeting these challenges will require a renewed commitment to research, innovation, and technology development in agriculture.. If we act strategically today we will gain invaluable benefits tomorrow, including enhanced food security, better nutrition, greener sources of energy, and healthier lives, while we grow the rural economy."[135] Daniel and his friends could start meeting these challenges by recommending that the president support legalizing industrial hemp.

The report then recorded that Barbara Schaal, co-chair of the PCAST Agricultural Preparedness Working Group said, "the challenges we face today, including long-term water security and the need for better integrated pest management strategies, involve public goods not easily monetized and are unlikely to be addressed by the private sector", this is where the report is way off base. Our well-intentioned politicians are not realizing that they are prohibiting the private sector from using a plant that fulfills all of your "top priorities."[136] They are also in denial that the overuse of water and the degradation of waterways is a direct result of government water subsidies and government intervention.

Decentralizing the farming industry was also brought up when the report mentioned that 60% of the grant funding goes to research done by government researchers. This is compared to 30% in other federal agencies. To go along with the need to allocate funds more effectively, the report recommended that the budget's focus should be shifted away from "corn, soy, rice, wheat, and cotton."[137] Hemp activists aren't asking for any government handout, we're just asking that the government start respecting what the citizens want and demand.

HempStrong's vision for more efficient water usage is tied directly to the plant that we were founded to promote. Just by legalizing industrial hemp farmers will be given the opportunity to improve their soil while growing one of the lowest water demanding cash crops in the world.

To better understand just how crops use water the organization waterfootprint.org has broken water into three separate categories green water, blue water, and grey water. Green water is refers to rain water that irrigates crops, blue water comes from the diversion of water flows or groundwater pumping, and grey water is the wastewater that is created from growing a crop or producing a product. The water that we are most interested in is blue water consumption. In almost all circumstances blue water consumption is unsustainable. The massive Ogallala aquifer that supplies a large portion of Midwest farms with water is being depleted 20 times faster than the water can be replenished. This groundwater pumping is unsustainable and will eventually have to be stopped. Some experts believe that within a decade certain areas in western Texas will be bone dry. Hemp isn't completely drought resistant, but after receiving adequate rainwater during the first few weeks of spring the plant's taproot allows it to reach water where many plants wouldn't be able. Hemp also grows at a very rapid pace and is extremely dense, this allows soil to stay cooler and slows the water evaporation rate from the soil.

Cotton (One of hemp's competitors) has been found to be one of the worst culprits when it comes to using unsustainable water practices and on average only 64% of its total water comes from sustainable rainwater. Cotton crops in American deserts and arid places all across the world have been getting water subsidies for years. California of all states looks to be one of the worst states when looking at blue water consumption in America. The largest blue water countries should be of no surprise and include India, China, USA, and Pakistan. These four countries also lead the globe in cotton exports and consequently the exportation of water via agricultural commodities. People need to realize that every time we export farm commodities we are diminishing our valuable water resources. As a country we need to make sure we are not exporting more water than we replenish.

Corn, wheat, rice and cotton not only use more water than hemp, but also use more agrochemicals. Organic hemp is in high demand in Canada and it is poised to take a large market share once it is legalized in America. Just by planting hemp farmers can improve their land and benefit water sheds all across the nation.

As you can see HempStrong hopes to have the biggest impact on the environment by changing how and what we farm, but this isn't our only strategy. We plan to raise the bar by making higher quality products and hope to influence our competitors by flipping industries upside down. We understand that most companies would be hesitant to get involved with the hemp industry due to its controversial cousin, but it is our job to lead the way and create real change.

Company's Vision

We cannot stay in business and accomplish our environmental vision without consistent profit. Short-term gains however will not be incorporated into our business philosophy. We believe it is more important to look at the consequences of our decisions 10, 15, and even 100 years down the road. We look at profit more as a measuring stick to gauge how well we are being accepted within our communities.

HempStrong sees our sustainability problems as a global issue and we hope to be able to reach all corners of the globe with our mission. As you now know America is the only industrialized country in the world that doesn't allow the cultivation of hemp. We believe that once America legalizes industrial hemp we will be able to lead the world in hemp innovation and turn a niche market into the most utilized crop on Earth. The sooner America can show the benefits of using hemp as a raw material, the sooner we can show developing countries how hemp can improve their economies. We plan on developing the hemp industry by creating strategic partnerships with our suppliers while developing new markets to be explored. We envision seeing our products in industries where you might not expect to see a sustainable product made from hemp.

To go along with being a company built around quality products, we also hope to be a difference maker in the world of education. We hope to not only educate our customers about the benefits of hemp, but we also want to keep our community up to date with the latest environmental, sustainability, and economic issues that are important to the HempStrong team and our customers.

At HempStrong Brands we exist to create sustainable products that create real value in people's lives. While starting HempStrong I knew I wouldn't be truly happy unless I was out in the real world solving real problems and creating real prosperity. I wanted to be a part of something bigger than myself and I wanted to create things that people fell in love with. HempStrong believes the solutions to our problems are simple and they are not as complex as the media and our political leaders would like you to think. We all just need to start working and living for the right reasons. Doing meaningful work is a must in order to secure a better tomorrow.

Innovation is at the heart of the HempStrong community and we will only enter markets that we feel we can significantly contribute. Helping to develop an industry that has pretty much been non-existent for the last 100 years is a big mountain to climb and we realize that our business strategy and vision may change very quickly. Collaboration with people outside of the HempStrong team will be essential for us to keep up with all that goes into developing an industry.

We believe that speaking with candor is important to the success of our business and establishing healthy friendships for the long-term. Walt Whitman said it best when he wrote in 1855, "The great poets are to be known by the absence in them of tricks, and by the justification of perfect personal candor. All faults may be forgiven of him who has perfect candor. Henceforth let no man of us lie, for we have seen that openness wins the inner and outer world, and that there is no single exception." HempStrong believes that its biggest asset will be the way we communicate with our employees and our community. We seek to create a working environment that prides itself on decentralization and empowers team members to make important decisions regarding the future of HempStrong and their careers. Each HempStrong team member will be given ample time to work on their own HempStrong projects and are free to collaborate with fellow team members on their own HempStrong ideas. We hope our openness to our community and our team will be rewarded with openness and candor coming from our customers and employees. We build our products for you and there is no reason why our customers shouldn't be more involved in critiquing our current products and influencing our future designs. We strive to establish a very unique and powerful relationship with our customers through as many channels as possible. Our hope is to have the most engaging & educated fans in world.

The Paradigm Shift

"Many people, especially ignorant people, want to punish you for speaking the truth, for being correct, for being you. Never apologize for being correct, or for being years ahead of your time. If you're right and you know it, speak your mind. Even if you are a minority of one, the truth is still the truth." – Gandhi

Trying to fix our sustainability and economic problems within the same paradigm that got us into this mess will never create the necessary solutions and innovations needed to fix the root problem. To fix the problems we face as a nation and as a global community we must look outside of the established paradigms and look to create new ones.

You might be asking yourself what is a paradigm shift? Thomas Kuhn is known to have popularized the term in a book he wrote in 1962 called The Structure of Scientific Revolutions. A paradigm shift is simply a shift away from the status quo toward a new conceptual viewpoint of how we go about our lives and view the world. In his book Kuhn described that a paradigm shift is needed when stakeholders come across anomalies that do not jive with the current paradigm. As more and more anomalies surface the old paradigm enters a period of crisis, which eventually gives birth to new ideas, concepts, and theories. These ideas can be both old and new and will be experimented with until one gains new acceptance by the masses. Paradigm shifts can occur slowly over decades or occur over a short period of time. The bottom line is we don't need tweaks in failed government policies or tweaks in the way we currently do business, and we definitely don't need to be kicking the can down the road. We need a transformation, a different way of thinking, and a paradigm shift to usher in new ideas, concepts, and lifestyles. It is important to note that not all paradigm shifts are for the better and we can reasonably conclude that our previous paradigm shifts, (the one we are living in right now) have failed us in many ways.

When Copernicus announced that the Earth rotated around the Sun along with the rest of the planets he did not come to this conclusion by looking at prior theories. Copernicus came to his conclusion by looking at the problem in a different light. Trying to solve new problems in failed paradigms will only lead to confusion, frustration, and failure. As we look ahead to solve our future environmental, health, and economic problems we must do what Copernicus did and remove ourselves from failed paradigms.

We are currently in the middle of one of the biggest paradigm shifts for businesses since the industrial revolution and I don't know how one can't be excited about it. The focus of businesses, both big and small is being shifted away from just the bottom-line to a much more customer-focused attitude. This paradigm shift was born during the early ages of Internet and has now begun to blossom with development of social media. One of the biggest contributors to this shift in business has been Mark Zuckerburg, the founder of Facebook. Zuckerburg didn't invent social media, but he made it a mainstream issue and gave consumers a bigger voice to talk back to businesses. Prior to the social media frenzy, marketing was a one-way street. Previously businesses hired marketing firms to dictate the marketplace by pushing their brands onto the public through television spots and print ads. Now conscious consumers are constantly talking back via social media.

Consumers are now more likely to switch brands and tell all their friends via social media if a business begins to falter, move away from it's original mission, or has a decline in quality. In essence what the Internet and social media have accomplished has allowed the market to work more efficiently. The average consumer now has more say in how a business functions than ever before. Businesses can't simply dictate the marketplace anymore (unless they have people in the government supporting their mercantilist policies).

One problem that paradigm shifts face either in science, social, or business settings is that there tends to be pushback from those who are still benefiting from the status quo. People need to remember that current paradigms are in place because they received mass appeal in the past. They either worked in the past/current environment or just showed the illusion of working. To be successful in creating a more sustainable global economy we must begin to influence a paradigm shift in the sustainability of our supply chains. We believe industrial hemp and the move to a more decentralized economy are going to be important factors in developing our new paradigm. The current status quo is a failure and we must begin to put our best foot forward in our business and life decisions. We deserve better both environmentally and economically.

Since I have discovered the hemp industry I have recognized many trends that look encouraging to the hemp movement and the paradigm shift in sustainability. Many of these trends suggest a huge future for the most versatile plant on the planet. If hemp is going to be successful in influencing our paradigm shift we must encourage the growth of the following trends:

Going Green: As more men and women begin voting with their wallets we will begin to see more and more entrepreneurs enter the green marketplace. Early adaptors of green products and technologies will lead the way in influencing green businesses practices. The hemp industry is in a great position to benefit from this ever-growing trend.

Entrepreneurship: Green shoppers wouldn't have anything to buy if it wasn't for the vision of entrepreneurs and capital from investors. At HempStrong we strive to maintain a decentralized team of hard working entrepreneurs who are focused on solving our sustainability and health problems. In recent years the go green movement has caught the attention of many like-minded entrepreneurs who have begun to stress the importance of their social goals as much as their financial goals.

Social Media: I have already mentioned the benefits that social media could have creating our new business paradigm, but this trend can play a huge role in how fast we legalize industrial hemp. Social media is not just about being social; it is about learning and sharing information in a meaningful way. The faster people hear about our message, the easier it will be to influence public servants and thus reintroduce industrial hemp. Social media creates a great platform to speak from.

High Demand for Plant Fiber: As consumers begin to look for more sustainable alternatives the demand for high quality plant fiber is set to explode. Hemp is in a position to meet this high demand.

Organic Farming: Many farmers are beginning to actually see the damages caused by mono cropping and the abuse of agrochemicals. Organic farming can revitalize rural America and create a healthier environment for future generations. The hemp industry is totally behind the organic farming industry and we hope organic shoppers will see the benefit of legalizing industrial hemp.

<u>Buy Local:</u> The buy local campaign has created a whole new opportunity for entrepreneurs. Currently Americans can only buy imported hemp products, but by legalizing industrial hemp this could help decentralize production of hundreds of goods and eliminate a large chunk of transportation. By decentralizing our economy we will empower our small farmers and middle class citizens.

<u>Healthy Living:</u> The last few years many Americans have discovered the benefits of eating healthy and the importance of a healthy environment. Hemp cannot only be a nutritious snack, but could provide us with environmentally friendly consumer products that we use on a daily basis.

<u>Green Investment:</u> Green startups are attracting investors at a record pace. If your product can meet the requirements of a green consumer the money can be found.

As these trends continue to play out and merge together we are excited to see how they will support the hemp industry and the development of our new paradigm. Currently according to VoteHemp.com 19 states have passed legislation regarding industrial hemp. If you are interested in becoming more active in hemp legalization or want to know the status of your state please visit votehemp.com.

Grow Better

On our website (HempStrong.com) we have "Grow Better" as our tagline.

Grow Better can mean grow better as an individual, grow better as a family, grow better as a business, and most importantly grow better as a society. HempStrong believes that we should all constantly be growing better one step at a time. In this great world we live in we should all strive to keep learning, living, and love what we do everyday.

One of the most important ideas conscious consumers need to understand is that we aren't going to fix our problems over night. It's going to take years and decades of like-minded people moving in the right direction. At HempStrong our goal is to continue to grow better and to touch as many people as possible with our mission of growing a better world. We realize that no business is completely sustainable or will be sustainable for sometime. Quite simply we don't have the knowhow or the necessary technology to create 100% sustainable manufacturing at this point. However, we firmly believe that if governments provide the proper economic incentives we will be there sooner than your think. The last few decades we have been introduced to some of the most amazing products the world has ever seen. These products and new technologies have done more to create a sustainable world than we ever thought possible. Just think of all the devices and energy that is saved from using a smart phone. Even with all the problems we face as a global community we still are becoming a healthier, greener, and more efficient planet every year.

Many people don't realize that this trend in increased efficiency is just now being applied to environmental issues and this trend will continue to accelerate at a rapid pace. We have faith that efficiency and environmental problems will continue to improve simply by looking at what the customers are demanding. More and more customers are demanding eco-friendly products and there is a huge market out there for willing entrepreneurs to meet their demands.

As wealth in societies rise, people will spend more time and capital on tackling environmental problems. Generation Y remains the X-factor in how fast and efficiently we tackle our global problems. The men and women who are a part of this generation don't know what the world was like before we had Earth Day. We have real potential to push the issue of creating a more sustainable planet simply by using social media and applying our greatest asset, our minds toward fixing our problems.

We should all be optimistic about the future of our great planet and embrace changes that bring the world closer together. Technologies such as solar panels are making more economic sense each year and face-to-face chatting via Skype has the potential to decrease the need for business travel.

Grow Better doesn't just mean grow better with industrial hemp. As we already said we realize the hemp doesn't hold all the answers, but we believe it can play a vital role in many of the solutions. The *Grow Better* message should simply encompass everything we do on a daily basis. From our family to our work, we can all grow better at something.

In order to successfully complete our goals as a company we are going to need the help and collaboration from all or of our stakeholders. From our newest team member, to our first customer, to the politician who just got elected, we hope everybody can grow better with the HempStrong team and industrial hemp.

Scott Sondles

Notes

[1] Herodotus, *The Histories* B. 4: 71-76, trans. Aubrey de Sélincourt, ed. A. R. Burn, (Viking Penguin, Inc.: New York, 1972) pp. 294-295.
[2] "The Invention of Paper." *Robert C. Williams Paper Museum.* Robert C. Williams Paper Museum, n.d. Web. <http://www.ipst.gatech.edu/amp/collection/museum_invention_paper.htm>
[3] Snelling, Nick. "What Did The Moors Do For Us?" *What Did The Moors Do For Us?* N.p., n.d. Web. 24 Sept. 2012.
[4] Ibid.
[5] Kinsella, Susan. "Conservatree." *Conservatree.* N.p., n.d. Web. 24 Sept. 2012. <http://www.conservatree.org/learn/Papermaking/History.shtml>.
[6] "Oil Paint - History." *Oil Paint - History.* N.p., n.d. Web. 28 Jan. 2013. <http://www.cyberlipid.org/perox/oxid0011.htm>
[7] Bennett, Chris, Lynn Osburn, and Judy Osburn. "The Alchemist Monk Francois Rabelais." *The Alchemist Monk Francois Rabelais.* N.p., n.d. Web. 24 Sept. 2012. <http://www.alchemylab.com/cannabis_stone3.htm>.
[8] Hunter, David. "Hemp Paper Chronology."
[9] Clark, Victor Selden. *History of Manufacturers in the United States.* New York: Published for the Carnegie Institution of Washington by the McGraw-Hill Book, 1929.
[10] Ibid.
[11] Betts, Edwin M., ed. *Thomas Jefferson's Farm Book: With Commentary and Relevant Extracts from Other Writings.* Princeton: Princeton University Press, 1953. Rep. 1976, 1987, <u>1999</u>. Manuscript and transcription available online at http://www.thomasjeffersonpapers.org/farm/, 95.
[12] Smith, Adam. "Book II, Chapter 5." *Wealth Of Nations*
[13] Canavan, Kathy. "Ben Franklin –facts and Fallacies." *Ben FranklinÂ–facts and Fallacies.* N.p., 5 Nov. 2005. Web. 25 Sept. 2012. <http://www.udel.edu/PR/Messenger/04/04/ben.html>.
[14] Crosby, Alfred W. *America, Russia, Hemp, and Napoleon: American Trade with Russia and the Baltic, 1783-1812,.* [Columbus]: Ohio State UP, 1965. 53-54.
[15] Ibid. pg. 74.

[16] Ibid. pg. 79

[17] Ibid. pg. 101

[18] Ibid. pg. 110

[19] Ibid. pg. 114

[20] Ibid. pg. 128

[21] Ibid. pg. 144

[22] Ibid. pg. 172

[23] Ibid. pg. 179

[24] Ibid. pg. 207

[25] Hopkins, James F. *A History of the Hemp Industry in Kentucky.* N.p.: University of Kentucky, 1951.

[26] Ibid.

[27] Ibid.

[28] Ibid.

[29] Ibid.

[30] Ibid.

[31] Ibid.

[32] Ibid.

[33] Taussig, F. W. *The Tariff History of the United States.* New York: G.P. Putnam's Sons, 1931.

[34] Hopkins, James F. *A History of the Hemp Industry in Kentucky.* N.p.: University of Kentucky, 1951.

[35] Ibid.

[36] Taussig, F. W. *The Tariff History of the United States.* New York: G.P. Putnam's Sons, 1931.

[37] Hopkins, James F. *A History of the Hemp Industry in Kentucky.* N.p.: University of Kentucky, 1951.

[38] Ibid.

[39] Ibid.

[40] Taussig, F. W. *The Tariff History of the United States.* New York: G.P. Putnam's Sons, 1931.

[41] Ibid.

[42] Ibid.

[43] "Ludwig Von Mises Institute." *Panic of 1837.* N.p., n.d. Web. 12 Mar. 2013.

[44] Salerno, Joseph T. "An Austrian Taxonomy of Deflation—with Applications to the U.S." *The Quarterly Journal of Austrian Economics* 6.4 (2003): 81-109. Print.

[45] Hopkins, James F. *A History of the Hemp Industry in Kentucky.* N.p.: University of Kentucky, 1951.

[46] Ibid.

[47] Ibid.

[48] Petke, Fred. "Clark County's Agriculture Fate Could Rest in Hemp Legislation." *Central Kentucky News.* N.p., 25 Jan. 2013. Web. 29 Jan. 2013

[49] Lyster H. Dewey and Jason L. Merrill, "Hemp Hurds As Paper-Making Material," *United States Department of Agriculture Bulletin No. 404* (Washington D.C., October 14, 1916).

[50] *Yearbook of United States Agriculture,* 1917, in John Roulac, *Hemp Horizons* (White River Junction, Vermont: Chelsea Green Publishing Company, 1997), p. 35

[51] H.T. Nugent, "Report of Survey: Commercialized Hemp (1934–35 Crop) in the State of Minnesota," Memo to Harry J. Anslinger, Commissioner of Narcotics (Washington D.C., October 22, 1938). Reproduced in the Schaffer Drug Library, www.druglibrary.org/SCHAFFER/hemp/taxact/nugent1.htm.

[52] John Craig Lupien, "Unraveling an American Dilemma: The Demonization of Marihuana," Masters thesis prepared for the Division of Humanities of Pepperdine University, April 1995.

[53] Ibid.

[54] George A. Lower, "Flax and Hemp: From the Seed to the Loom," *Mechanical Engineering,* February 26, 1937;

[55] "New Billion-Dollar Crop," *Popular Mechanics,* February 1938.

[56] "Auschwitz:60 Year Anniversary-- the Role of IG Farben-Bayer." *Auschwitz:60 Year Anniversary-- the Role of IG Farben-Bayer.* N.p., 25 Jan. 2005. Web. 29 Jan. 2013. http://www.ahrp.org/infomail/05/01/27a.php

[57] "Auschwitz:60 Year Anniversary-- the Role of IG Farben-Bayer." *Auschwitz:60 Year Anniversary-- the Role of IG Farben-Bayer.* N.p., 25 Jan. 2005. Web. 29 Jan. 2013. <http://www.ahrp.org/infomail/05/01/27a.php>Ibid.

[58] Broughton, Philip D. "Forget Hitler - It Was America That Snubbed Black Olympian Jesse Owens." *Mail Online.* N.p., 11 Aug. 2009. Web. 29 Jan. 2013.

[59] Love, Philip H. *Andrew W. Mellon, the Man and His Work,.* Baltimore, MD: F.H. Coggins &, 1929. Print.

[60] Sennholz, Hans F. "The Great Depression." *The Ludwig Von Mises Institute.* N.p., 24 June 2009. Web. 10 Mar. 2013.

[61] Folsom, Burton W. *New Deal or Raw Deal?* New York: Threshold Editions, 2008. 53. Print.

[62] Ibid.

[63] Ibid.

[64] Morris, David. "Hydrocarbons vs Carbohydrates: The Continuing Battle in the United States." *Hydrocarbons vs Carbohydrates: The Future of Plastics.* The Institute for Local Self-Reliance, n.d. Web. 05 Apr. 2013.

[65] "Did You Know?" *Hemp History Week -.* N.p., n.d. Web. 25 Jan. 2013. <http://hemphistoryweek.com/didyouknow.php>

[66] *Single Convention on Narcotic Drugs, 1961*, Article 28-2.

[67] David P. West, "Hawai`i Industrial Hemp Research Project Final Report," memo to Lee D. Donohue,Chief of Police, City and County of Honolulu, Hawaii (December 12, 2003).

[68] "Sourcebook of Criminal Justice Statistics." N.p., n.d. Web. http://www.albany.edu/sourcebook/pdf/t4382005.pdf

[69] "New Hampshire Hemp council Inc v. Marshal.", *No.Ã¢Â€Â,99-1082., January 28, 2000.* N.p., n.d. Web. 21 July 2012. <http://caselaw.findlaw.com/us-1st-circuit/1153595.html>.

[70] Smith-Heisters, Skaidra. "Environmental Costs of Hemp Prohibition in the United States." *Journal of Industrial Hemp* 13.2 (2008):

[71] Jean M. Rawson, *Hemp as an Agricultural Commodity* (Washington D.C.: Congressional Research Service, July 8, 2005), p. 3.

[72] Smith-Heisters, Skaidra. "Environmental Costs of Hemp Prohibition in the United States." *Journal of Industrial Hemp* 13.2 (2008): 157-70.

[73] Roulac, John. *Hemp Horizons: The Comeback of the World's Most Promising Plant.* White River Junction, VT: Chelsea Green Pub., 1997. Pg 97.

[74] N. Cherret et al., "Ecological Footprint and Water Analysis of Cotton, Hemp and Polyester: Report prepared for and reviewed by BioRegional Development Group and World Wide Fund for Nature, Cymru" (Stockholm, Sweden: Stockholm Environment Institute, 2005).

[75] A.K. Chapagain et al., "The water footprint of cotton consumption," *Value of Water: Research Report Series*, no. 18

(UNESCO-IHE Institute for Water Education: September2005).

[76] "Cotton and the Environment." - *Organic Trade Association*. N.p., n.d. Web. 23 Nov. 2012. http://www.ota.com/organic/environment/cotton_environment.h tml

[77] Chouinard, Yvon, and Vincent Stanley. *The Responsible Company*. Ventura, CA: Patagonia, 2012. Print. Pg. 49.

[78] Agriculture, United States Department of. "Cotton Production Statistics - Countries Compared - Nationmaster." *NationMaster.com*. NationMaster, n.d. Web. 19 July 2012. <http://www.nationmaster.com/red/pie/agr_cot_pro-agriculture-cotton-production>.

[79] David Pimentel, "Environmental and Economic Costs of the Application of Pesticides Primarily in the United States," *Environment, Development and Sustainability*, vol. 7, no. 2 (June 2005).

[80] "Cotton and the Environment." - *Organic Trade Association*. N.p., n.d. Web. 23 Nov. 2012. http://www.ota.com/organic/environment/cotton_environment.h tml

[81] Edward Humes, Force of Nature (New York: HaperCollins, 2011), 126-127.

[82] "Cotton and the Environment." - *Organic Trade Association*. N.p., n.d. Web. 23 Nov. 2012. http://www.ota.com/organic/environment/cotton_environment.h tml

[83] Chouinard, Yvon, and Vincent Stanley. *The Responsible Company*. Ventura, CA: Patagonia, 2012. Print. Pg. 51.

[84] Cotton and the Environment." - *Organic Trade Association*. N.p., n.d. Web. 23 Nov. 2012. http://www.ota.com/organic/environment/cotton_environment.h tml

[85] Palmer, Brian. "Can Hemp Clothing save the Planet?" *Slate Magazine*. N.p., 12 Apr. 2011. Web. 23 Nov. 2012. <http://www.slate.com/articles/health_and_science/the_green_lan tern/2011/04/high_on_environmentalism.single.html>.

[86] *BBC News.* BBC, 16 Mar. 2000. Web. 23 Nov. 2012.
<http://news.bbc.co.uk/2/hi/asia-pacific/678898.stm>
[87] Mekonnen, M. M., and A. Y. Hoekstra. "The Green, Blue and Grey Water Footprint of Crops and Derived Crop Products." *Hydrology and Earth System Sciences* 5 (2011): n. pag. Print
[88] Freinkel, Susan. *Plastic: A Toxic Love Story.* Boston: Houghton Mifflin Harcourt, 2011.
[89] Goodall, Christine. "Bioplastics: An Important Component of Global Sustainability." *Biome Bioplastics* (2011)
[90] Ibid.
[91] Quoted in European Plastics News, July 26th 2011.
http://www.europeanplasticsnews.com/subscriber/headlines2.html?cat=1&id=1311674045
[92] Dow Chemical expects its proposed Brazilian bio-polyethylene plant to produce plastic at about the same cost as the oil-based equivalent.
http://www.technologyreview.com/energy/38114/
[93] Goodall, Christine. "Bioplastics: An Important Component of Global Sustainability." *Biome Bioplastics* (2011)
[94] "National Bioeconomy Blueprint Released." *The White House.* N.p., 26 Apr. 2012. Web. 12 Dec. 2012.
[95] Wambua, Paul, Jan Ivens, and Ignaas Verpoest. "Natural Fibres: Can They Replace Glass in Fibre Reinforced Plastics?" *Composites Science and Technology* 63.9 (2003): 1259-264. Print.
[96] Amaducci, S., M. T. Amaducci, R. Benati, and G. Venturi. "Crop Yield and Quality Parameters of Four Annual Fibre Crops (hemp, Kenaf, Maize and Sorghum) in the North of Italy." *Industrial Crops and Products* (1999): n. pag. Print.
[97] Hashim, Jamil. "On the Effect of Abrasiveness to Process Equipment Using Betelnut and Glass Fibres Reinforced Polyester Composites." *Wear* 290-291 (2012): n. pag. Print.
[98] Peter A. Nelson, "Performance-Based Industrial Hemp Fiber Will Propel New Technologies in the 21st Century," *The Vote Hemp Report* (2002/2003), p. 21.
[99] Belcher (2001) and Mehta (2003) in L. T. Drzal et al., Michigan State University, "Biobased Structural Composite Materials for Housing and Infrastructure Applications: Opportunities and Challenges," NSF-PATH Housing Research Agenda Workshop, Proceedings and Recommendations, (2004), pp. 129-140.

[100] "Lotus Group." *Eco Elise.* N.p., n.d. Web. 03 Aug. 2012. <http://www.lotuscars.com/gb/engineering/eco-elise>.

[101] Pearson, Paul, and Everett Swift. "Michigan Hemp Report, Hemp for the Automotive Industry." (n.d.): n. pag.

[102] Ibid.

[103] "Auto Body Made of Plastics Resists Denting Under Hard Blows." *Popular Mechanics Magazine* 76.6 (1941)

[104] Hunt, Kasie. "GOP Senate Leader Mitch McConnell Supports Bill to Legalize Hemp Production." *NBC News.* N.p., n.d. Web. 01 Mar. 2013.

[105] Walsh, Diane. "Canada's Herbal Remedy to the Auto Crisis: The Kestrel Hemp EV." - *Salem-News.Com.* N.p., 17 Jan. 2011. Web. 03 Aug. 2012. <http://www.salem-news.com/articles/january172011/hemp-car-dw.php>.

[106] Joshi, S.v, L.t Drzal, A.k Mohanty, and S. Arora. "Are Natural Fiber Composites Environmentally Superior to Glass Fiber Reinforced Composites?" *Composites Part A: Applied Science and Manufacturing* 35.3 (2004): 371-76.

[107] Buckley, Christine. "Current Research." *UConn Biofuel Consortium.* N.p., n.d. Web. 04 Dec. 2012. <http://biodiesel.engr.uconn.edu/research.html>

[108] "Natural Fibers and Recycled Plastics Form New Building Material | College of Engineering Newsletter | UNC Charlotte." *Natural Fibers and Recycled Plastics Form New Building Material | College of Engineering Newsletter | UNC Charlotte.* N.p., n.d. Web. 20 July 2012. <http://coe.uncc.edu/newsletter/2011-spring/127-natural-fibers-and-recycled-plastics-form-new-building-material.html>.

[109] Ibid.

[110] Lime Technology, (2010).

[111] Ibid.

[112] *Limetalk* (Summer 2011): n. pag.

[113] "Fast Facts â€" Behind the Numbers | Concrete Joint Sustainability Initiative." *Fast Facts â€" Behind the Numbers.* N.p., n.d. Web. 15 Dec. 2012.

[114] "What Is Hemp Insulation?" *CanFIber.* N.p., n.d. Web. 15 Dec. 2012.

[115] "Research Team Develops Faux Wood That Can Biodegrade." *Standford News.* N.p., 18 Mar. 2009. Web. 16 Dec. 2012.

[116] *Tradical® Hemcrete® Designer's Information Pack.* Oxfordshire: Lime Technology, n.d. Print.

[117] "The Environment." *Hemp Technology Ltd: Resources.* N.p., n.d. Web. 15 Dec. 2012.

[118] Herer, Jack, and Leslie Cabarga. *The Emperor Wears No Clothes.* [Calif.]: Ah Ha Pub., 1998.

[119] "Living Tree Paper | Paper & Environment." *Living Tree Paper | Paper & Environment.* N.p., n.d. Web. 31 Dec. 2012.

[120] "Living Tree Paper | Pulp & Paper Facts." *Living Tree Paper | Pulp & Paper Facts.* N.p., n.d. Web. 31 Dec. 2012.

[121] Lucht, Gene. "Water Quality Program Detailed to Farm Bureau." *Iowa Farmer Today.* N.p., 13 Dec. 2012. Web. 30 Dec. 2012.

[122] Ibid.

[123] Baxter, W.J. "Growing Industrial Hemp in Ontario." *Growing Industrial Hemp in Ontario.* N.p., Aug. 2009. Web. 30 Dec. 2012.

[124] Ibid.

[125] Harrison, Brandy. "Company Aims to Boost Hemp in Eastern Ontario and Quebec to 10,000 Acres by 2014." *Farmers Forum.* N.p., Nov. 2012. Web. 23 Apr. 2013.

[126] "History of Hemp in Chile." *History of Hemp in Chile.* N.p., n.d. Web. 01 Jan. 2013.

[127] Ibid.

[128] Brown, David. "China Leads the World for Hemp Fabrics." *Examiner.com.* N.p., 17 June 2010. Web. 01 Jan. 2013.

[129] Ibid.

[130] Roulac, John. *Hemp Horizons: The Comeback of the World's Most Promising Plant.* White River Junction, VT: Chelsea Green Pub., 1997.

[131] Source: Health Canada website, at: http://www.hc-sc.gc.ca/dhpmps/pubs/precurs/factsheet_fiche_e.html

[132] "USDA ERS - Irrigation & Water Use." *USDA ERS - Irrigation & Water Use.* N.p., 19 July 2012. Web. 07 Dec. 2012.

[133] "Running Dry." *The Economist.* The Economist Newspaper, 18 Sept. 2008. Web. 07 Dec. 2012.

[134] Weiss, Rick. "Presidential Report Calls for New "Innovation Ecosystem" for Agricultural Research." *TheWhitehouse.* The Government, 7 Dec. 2012. Web. 9 Dec. 2012.

[135] Ibid.

[136] Ibid.

[137] Ibid

31073933R10097

Made in the USA
Middletown, DE
28 December 2018